X06

NO GARLIC IN THE SOUP!

Adult Books by LEONARD WIBBERLEY

MRS. SEARWOOD'S SECRET WEAPON
THE MOUSE THAT ROARED
MCGILLICUDY MCGOTHAM
THE TROUBLE WITH THE IRISH
TAKE ME TO YOUR PRESIDENT
BEWARE OF THE MOUSE
COMING OF THE GREEN
NO GARLIC IN THE SOUP!

Juvenile Books by PATRICK O'CONNOR
(pseudonym)

THE SOCIETY OF FOXES
FLIGHT OF THE PEACOCK
THE WATERMELON MYSTERY
GUNPOWDER FOR WASHINGTON
THE LOST HARPOONER
THE FIVE-DOLLAR WATCH MYSTERY
THE BLACK TIGER
MEXICAN ROAD RACE
BLACK TIGER AT LE MANS

Juvenile Books by LEONARD WIBBERLEY

THE KING'S BEARD
CORONATION BOOK
DEADMAN'S CAVE
EPICS OF EVEREST
WOUND OF PETER WAYNE
LIFE OF WINSTON CHURCHILL
THE SECRET OF THE HAWK
KEVIN O'CONNOR AND THE LIGHT BRIGADE
JOHN BARRY, FATHER OF THE NAVY
WES POWELL: CONQUEROR OF THE GRAND CANYON

NO GARLIC
in the
SOUP!

LEONARD WIBBERLEY

Illustrated by ERNIE MELCHIOR

IVES WASHBURN, INC.
New York

Contents

NO GARLIC IN THE SOUP!

The Great Decision

1.   WHEN A MAN DECIDES TO TAKE
his wife, his four children, his bulldog, his automobile, and
about sixteen pieces of baggage to Portugal to live for an in-
definite period, he certainly ought to have good reason for so
doing.

Perhaps the oddest part of my decision to go to Portugal is
that I hadn't a good reason. I tried very hard to find one and
did a great deal of utterly spurious rationalization in my search
for a motive.

But the candid fact is that I was simply obsessed with an
overpowering desire to go to Portugal, as a man may be over-
taken in the oddest moment by a strong urge to eat a banana
split. In a sense a Portuguese ghost was haunting me and would
not leave me be. I would set about writing a children's book,
and into the pages would march some reference to Portugal
or some character from Portugal demanding recognition.

I would go down to San Pedro harbor to sail and would see
the fleets of fishing boats manned by Portuguese and reflect
that nobody really knows very much about the Portuguese.
Between Vasco da Gama and Dr. António de Oliveira Salazar,
Portugal is a big blank for most of us.

Or I would go into the supermarket, and at the counter
where all the odd varieties of canned fish are kept in their
curiously shaped tins I would find a stack of canned sardines
from Portugal.

So one day I decided that we must all go to Portugal, and I told my wife about this decision.

"Hazel," I said, "let's sell the house and go to Portugal."

Hazel at that time was pregnant, our baby being due in about four months.

"Okay," she said.

Having reached so drastic a decision, it was necessary to supply ourselves with sensible reasons for our actions—partly so that we could pretend we were acting in a sensible manner and partly to satisfy the curiosity of friends and business acquaintances who could hardly be expected to be satisfied with the explanation that I was haunted by a Portuguese ghost.

The sensible reasons, none of which deceived either of us for a moment, ran as follows:

a) It was ridiculous for a writer whose income is at best haphazard to continue to struggle for a living in a country where living costs are as high as they are in the United States. Any reasonable writer would go to live in a country such as Portugal where living costs are lower. People, however, kept asking, "Why Portugal?" when Mexico, for example, is but a few score miles from southern California, where we lived, and living costs there are remarkably low. To this we could only reply that we were going to Portugal because nobody ever seemed to go there. In its great days Portugal had discovered much of the world, but the world had not yet returned the compliment and discovered Portugal. We proposed to do so.

b) Life in the United States had settled into a routine of work and entertainment that no longer entertained. I personally got my greatest weekly enjoyment out of going to the local supermarket, which, with its mounds of green, yellow, red, and purple fruits, its clean shelves of glittering canned goods, its exciting meat counter and stacks of such fascinating merchandise as dish drainers, mops, fat cans of floor polish, bottles of soft drinks and fruit juices, is, for me, an Aladdin's cave of treasures. But even the supermarket was beginning to pall. Furthermore, every time I went there it cost thirty dollars or so, and I maintained that for thirty dollars I could live handsomely for a week in some other country—especially Portugal.

c) An author, by the traditions of his profession, should be a cosmopolitan man. Southey visited Lisbon, Dickens went to Italy, Hemingway lives in Cuba and has spent many years in France and Spain. Somerset Maugham moves as readily around the world as if each country were but a room in his house. What, then, was the matter with Wibberley plodding in his slippers to the supermarket for his pleasures? Had he not also an equal right as an author to view Capri and Madrid, and would not the very best place to start upon this more proper and fuller literary life be Portugal?

I liked this argument best myself, for there is a touch of snobbery to my nature, and though timidly disposed, I like to fancy myself an international traveler, a cosmopolite, and perhaps something of an expert on Venetian glass or Dresden china—subjects of which I know nothing.

d) The final reason we dredged up was that travel would be good for the children. There was some substance to this reason, for we are anxious that our children should not, because of a narrow nationalism, despise the people of other countries, or hold themselves superior to them because of the geographical accident of birth. It would do Kevin, for instance, good, to collect a black eye and a friend in some Portuguese village. . . . It would be helpful to Patricia and to Christopher and to Arabella to meet their counterparts in other lands.

And so we put our house up for sale and started to make inquiries about passage.

Selling the house wasn't really hard. People wandered into it silently, looking at the floor and the ceiling and opening the cupboards as if they were examining some curious dwelling from a long-forgotten civilization. But after a couple of months of these ghostlike visitors the right couple walked in and announced that they would like to buy the place, and so the deed was done.

What really gave us trouble was getting out of the house. By that I mean deciding what stuff to junk, what stuff to sell, what stuff to put in storage, and what stuff to forward to Portugal. There was a lot of stuff. I personally counted three hundred and twenty-four brown paper bags that Hazel had brought back from the grocery and which she had saved because there was some fear in the back of her mind that one day she would be in desperate need of a vast quantity of brown paper bags.

There was also perhaps a ton and a half of assorted children's toys or parts of children's toys. I would estimate twenty small cars each lacking a wheel or two and a like number of dolls and stuffed toy animals such as bears and dogs and so on with missing limbs, eyes, or ears, or in some way maimed.

There were enough guns to have tamed the West in the 1860's and a dozen holsters and gun belts that had seen service in many a battle (around the house) between the United States cavalry and the Sioux, though sometimes these battles were between the United States Marines and the Japanese.

There were roller skates without straps on them and tennis rackets bent to the shape of ill-treated snowshoes. There were thrilling boxes of colored beads, which I decided to save because I like colored beads, and there were masses of bobbins

with black, white, red, green, turquoise, pink, and yellow
thread on them. The children wanted to take every single toy,
for they loved each one dearly, and Christopher, who was
almost five, particularly loved a black rubber hunting knife
that looked like an adder's tongue. He had, I suppose, stabbed
many a foe to death with it and could not readily part with
so trusty a weapon.

He stuffed it into the pocket of his jeans and glowered at
me defiantly.

"I'm taking my good old knife," he said.

"There're no Indians in Portugal," I said.

"There are, too, Indians in Portugal," said Christopher.
"Aren't there, Mother?" And his mother agreed that there
certainly were. Actually, of course, for boys of five, the whole
world is populated with Indians as well as grizzly bears, and
a very fine world it is, too. And so the knife came with us.

Clothes I left to my wife. "Pack only what is needed," I
said, "bearing in mind that clothing is commonly to be had in
all parts of the world and at a reasonable price. That goes for
bedclothes, too."

When I went over the clothing that was to be sent to the
Goodwill Industries I found a couple of fishing shirts of mine
without which I would refuse to enter even the gates of
heaven. I demanded that these be taken with us, brushing aside
niggling objections about the shirts being in need of mending
and having a sad odor of moribund fish. This was an error,
for the children then produced jeans and shoes and shirts and
other items that were to have been discarded and to which they
had some especial attachment. All these, then, went back into
the trunks so that we had a grand total of sixteen large trunks
into which I later discovered had been smuggled a number of

broken cars, guns, holsters, and disreputable dolls previously consigned to the junk yard.

On dishes, however, I was adamant.

"Not a dish or a cooking utensil," I said, "accompanies us to Portugal."

I was wrong, however, for we were accompanied to Portugal by a heavy iron skillet that Hazel managed to put in the trunk of the car. I still don't know why she brought it along and she refuses to discuss the matter. But I fancy the reason had something to do, perhaps, with being wrecked on a desert island and faced with the task of frying fish for a husband and four children—though it would likely be five by then.

Our friends took a glum view of the whole venture. It was gradually revealed to me that we in America have come to the conclusion that wholesome food is hardly to be had outside of the United States, that sanitation is unheard of in the howling and foreign darkness beyond our continental limits, and that the benefits of medicine extend no farther than the borders and coast lines of this nation.

"What about milk?" people would say to me with some concern, and when I replied that cows flourished in many parts of the world, and Pasteur had been a Frenchman, they would not cheer up at all, but remained of the opinion that all milk outside of America is full of death-dealing bugs.

The fact that Hazel would have her baby in foreign parts was the subject of much anxious discussion among her friends. It is pretty well accepted that babies are born in other countries (though Mother's Day is an American institution), and therefore there must be obstetricians and doctors of some degree of knowledge and skill in other lands. And yet the view seemed to prevail that babies and mothers die by the hundredfold unless attended by American physicians in American hospitals. There were vague forebodings about the use of anesthetics and antiseptics, but Hazel, who is psychic, was more disturbed about getting marine insurance for our car—a Rover and a very fine car indeed.

"You really ought to get some marine insurance," she said. "You can never tell."

"You can never tell what?" I asked.

"You can never tell when you might need marine insurance."

"I can tell that I wouldn't need marine insurance in the middle of the Mojave Desert," I replied.

"I mean if something happened to the ship," said Hazel.

"Look," I said, "if anything happens to the ship, the least of my worries, while floundering around in the water looking for you, the four kids, the bulldog, sixteen pieces of luggage, and a lifeboat would be whether I had marine insurance on Rover."

But knowing that Hazel is psychic, I bought a small water-proof plastic bag in which to keep cigarettes because it has appeared from my reading that the sufferings of the ship-wrecked are greatly increased by all the cigarettes getting wet.

When we had packed our personal stuff and thrown away, given away, or sold all else that we did not require, we called a moving company to pack the rest for storage. Two men arrived with a large van, a stack of collapsible cardboard cartons, and a three months' supply of daily newspapers.

"I want you to pack everything in the house and put it in storage," I said.

"Everything?" asked one of the men. He wore glasses.

"Everything except what's in this drawer here," I said, pointing.

They started packing and went at it like those locusts who devoured the first plantings of the Mormons. It was fascinating to watch how item after item was snatched up, swaddled in a sheet of newspaper, and thrust into a cardboard carton.

At noon the men decided to have lunch.

"Let's eat," said one.

"Okay," replied the other. "Where're my glasses?" He groped hopelessly around, and a look of misery came into his face.

"I guess I must have packed them," he said. After opening four cartons, they found the glasses. This gave me some stirrings of unease, and I inquired of Hazel, keeping my voice as steady and casual as I might, where our passports were. We had put them in the drawer which I had asked should not be touched. The drawer was empty and so we settled down to opening more of the cardboard cartons, undoing the morning's work. We found not only our passports but also our steamship tickets and a royalty check for no small sum. Where should we keep these items to save them from the locusts?

I put them in a jacket, but having hung the jacket in a closet, discovered a little later that the jacket had been packed, for the packers worked in a species of trance, disposing of all they came across. When we opened some of the cartons later, we found that they had packed several sticks of chewing gum which had by then lain in storage for almost a year. To save our essential travel documents, I finally put them in the cubbyhole of Rover and there they were secure.

At last the day to leave arrived. We planned to drive at a leisurely pace from California to New York by way of Florida. We loaded the four children into the car and loaded the trunk and luggage rack above with our bags. Rover is a small car as American cars are reckoned, but is a sturdy one and willing, and we trundled confidently out on the highway to nearby Los Angeles.

Los Angeles to Lisbon; that was the project, and we all felt quite adventurous. All except Christopher, that is.

"I want to stay with Craigie," he moaned, Craigie being his special friend.

I felt like a wretch but put my foot on the accelerator and struck up a stave or two of "Fire Down Below"—always a great favorite in my family—in the hopes of raising the spirits of all hands.

Portugal had called long enough and we were on our way,

fully equipped with all that was needed for such an enterprise, including Christopher's small rubber knife for despatch-
ing Indians, Hazel's skillet in case of being cast away on a
desert island, and a potty chair for Arabella which rode with
a continental dash atop the luggage rack. It was to plague me
considerably in the months ahead.

The Shipwrecked Rover

2.

THOSE WHO WISH TO DO ANY extensive traveling about the world should take their children with them. Lacking children of their own, they would be well advised to borrow a few from their friends or from some local orphanage. For children, far from being a great nuisance when traveling, increase the delights of the journey. They add a depth of perception which the adult is likely to miss and they are great enliveners of otherwise tedious hours spent behind the wheel of an automobile.

It was, for instance, from my son Christopher that I got a swift insight into the character of modern poetry. All the children, except Arabella who at the age of eighteen months was incapable of the attempt, were writing or pretending to write letters to their friends. Kevin, eight, could write reasonably well. Patricia, six, was learning fast. But Christopher at five could produce only a few ill-formed letters, quite as beautiful to him as a poem by Herrick would be to me.

When he had covered a page with such writing, he announced that his letter was finished.

"Is it a good letter?" I asked.

"Yes. But it's not very long."

"What does it say?"

"I don't know," said Christopher. "All I did was write it."

I marked him down as a latter-day poet on the moment.

We passed many curiosities on the road to New York but

surely none more curious than the western American pre-
occupation with reptiles. To judge by the roadside signs the
American West raises more snakes than cattle. For hundreds
of miles the highways are pocked with yellow signboards on
which, in black lettering, the approach of a giant reptile ranch
is announced.

"Gila Monsters—Educational," one sign read. "Twenty-foot
boa constrictor—clean restrooms," screamed another, while a
third demanded that all who passed, stop to see "the cobra that
killed Grace Wiley." Who was Grace Wiley? What peculiar
fate demanded that she should die in New Mexico of a cobra
probably hatched in India? The novelist is forbidden the use
of such bizarre material but is it not fascinating that an American girl named Grace Wiley should have met with an Indian
cobra, that the two should have been filled with loathing for
each other on sight with the result that Grace Wiley died and
the cobra became famous?

There were other sights of interest on the western roads—
black, hairy tarantulas tiptoeing in herds from one side of the
highway to another, all of them males, I believe, answering a
mating call from black hairy females in the farther bushes; a
positive litter of dead skunks extending most of the way across
Texas; and innumerable desert tortoises, lying upon the road
like boulders, their wise yet evil heads pulled nervously into
their shells.

In Louisiana, draped with its widows' weeds of Spanish
moss, we saw Negro women fishing in the roadside bayous
using live frogs for bait (the frogs, hooked through the mouth,
grasp piteously at the hook with their tiny hands), and in
Florida we met road gangs of convicts working under the
supervision of guards armed with shotguns. This had a most
depressing effect on the children, who wanted to know why

the men were compelled to work in this way and whether they would be shot and whether they did not miss their wives and children.

Finally we reached New York City, spent a day or two in a hotel, and then prepared to go aboard the vessel which was to carry us to Portugal. Since we were taking Rover with us, it was necessary to deliver the car to the dock by noon of the day before sailing, and this was done.

The following morning we arrived at the dock ourselves, sixteen pieces of luggage, four children, two adults, two violins, and a bulldog (though some of the luggage had, of course, been sent ahead to the ship).

The only piece of luggage I refused to be associated with was Arabella's potty chair, and I had conspired to leave this in the back of the car when I delivered it the previous day.

We were greeted by a lugubrious gentleman posted at the entrance to the pier with the purpose of picking us out from all the other passengers.

"Do you belong to that little Limey car?" he asked.

The question nettled me, for Rover is a family friend and has stood between us and the bears of Yellowstone National Park, among other services.

"If you mean the seventy-five-horsepower, six-cylinder Rover with an F head and twin SU carburetors," I replied, "yes."

"They dropped it," said the lugubrious gentleman.

"It's no little Limey car," I continued heatedly. "It will cruise all day at seventy miles an hour and has real leather upholstery . . ."

"Fell right out of the sling," said the man.

"And has a pressurized cooling system and . . . What did you say?"

"They dropped it. It's a bit bent," said the man.

"You mean they dropped my car?"

"That's what I've been telling you," said the man. "It's up on the dock. Baggagemaster wants to know whether you still want to load it."

"Here," I said to Hazel, and gave her two violins and the bulldog and raced upstairs.

There was Rover—the bentest car I have ever seen and I'm a veteran of newspaper reporting. The radiator was bent around the fan which was bent around the engine block. The hood was bent back toward the windshield, which was so bent it had broken. The front wheels were bent so that they were three feet out of place under the engine, and the back wheels were the shape of carelessly laid eggs. The doors were bent open and the dashboard was bent and so was the steering column and the steering wheel. I got down on my hands and knees, more or less to relieve my nerves, and noted that the box frame of the car was bent, too. A little arterial oil, thick and desperate, formed a glum pool under the crankcase, which was also bent.

"How did this happen?" I demanded.

"Like I said," answered the man; "they dropped it."

"Cripes," I said. "You just don't drop a car. Something goes wrong. Did the crane break or something?"

"Nope," replied the man. "They picked it up and slung it round and tried to stop it over the deck but she kept on going and fell right out of the nets and hit the dock. Happens all the time," he added. "They dropped a new Merc in the river last week."

"I suppose," I said, "that the bottom of the Hudson River is paved with automobiles that you guys dropped while loading ships."

He ignored that, or maybe he was used to such cracks.

"You ought to see the baggagemaster about it," he advised.

So I went to see the baggagemaster. This gentleman had troubles of his own. A lady was shipping a couple of guinea hens to Athens and was concerned that there should be enough guinea-hen food aboard to last through the voyage. She was also giving him instructions on the watering of guinea fowl while passing through the Mediterranean. I waited patiently.

The next gentleman in line had a dog problem, and the third was concerned about a bag which was lost somewhere among the scores of thousands of bags that formed the major cargo of the ship. By the time I got to the baggagemaster I was beginning to feel sorry for him.

"You've come about your car?" he said. "Do you wish us to ship it? I can still get it aboard for you."

"How do I know whether I should ship it or not?" I demanded. "I don't even know whether it can be repaired. I don't know, if it can be repaired, whether there are mechanics in Lisbon of sufficient skill and training to repair it. It looks like a total wreck to me."

"You have insurance?" the baggagemaster asked.

And suddenly I realized that I hadn't insurance. Hazel had been psychic and knew that something of this sort was going to happen, had warned me, and all I had done was buy a plastic bag to keep my cigarettes dry in case of shipwreck.

"No," I said, "I haven't got any insurance to cover an automobile being dropped from a crane while being put aboard a ship. I don't know what kind of insurance companies write that sort of insurance. It's a peculiar thing to happen to a car—like being torpedoed."

The baggagemaster smiled and reached into his pocket and drew out a cigarette case. "Have a cigarette," he said.

I took it. It wasn't much. But it was something.

"Well," he said, "when you've looked it over you might let me know whether you want to ship it or not."

"I've looked it over and it is completely wrecked," I replied. "We'd better leave it here until I can have the damage assessed and find out whether there is a garage in Lisbon at which it can be repaired."

"You'll get a new car," said the baggagemaster.

At that moment the sun rose as far as I was concerned. I went back to Hazel. The children were all crying because they loved Rover and Tully, the bulldog, had made a serious attempt to bite several of the porters.

"It's okay, kids," I said. "We're going to get a new car." The crying stopped instantly, but Tully, who is not readily deceived, continued to snap at the porters.

It is no simple matter to get aboard a tourist ship. Movies have popularized the notion that you arrive at the dockside, are presented with a wreath of flowers and several rolls of paper ribbons, obsequious porters take your baggage up the gangplank, and you follow, leaving time for a decent interval in which to consume a glass of champagne all around before sailing.

It doesn't happen like that, though. The whole passenger list stood in line for some hours on the dock, freezing, nervous, and irritable, or freezing, patient, and resigned, according to their separate natures, while their baggage statements were examined. We stood in this line, too, with Tully still snapping at any handy porters who soon learned to give him a wide berth. The children stood looking at the ship, of which we could see only a portion through a huge doorway, and kept inquiring whether it would sail without us. Tricia was still mad because the ship, in her view, had wrecked Rover, and she threw a paper bag containing the remains of an ice-cream cone at it, but caused no damage. Arabella wet twice and had to be twice changed, bawling blue murder, and Tully wet once and was clouted for this ill behavior.

Finally I got fed up. I am a man who will not stand readily in line even for his own death, and I didn't think it right that Hazel, heavy with child, should be put through this ordeal. So I got hold of one of the minor officials of the shipping company and told him I thought it was a pretty poor show to keep her standing in her condition. He agreed, and we were swept, earning the hate of our fellow passengers, up to the chief official examining the baggage. He passed us with a nod. We then went to another official who had to look at our tickets and passports and vaccination certificates, and after this we were allowed on board.

The ship we had elected to travel on was Greek. I think I chose a Greek ship because I have never eaten fried octopus and I had read somewhere that the Greeks are fond of this dish and serve it frequently. The vessel was newly built for the tourist trade, and had only a small first class, the rest of the accommodations being tourist class. We were traveling tourist and had seen, in a bewildering diagram, the two cabins allotted to us. They looked remarkably small but we were assured by the travel agent they would be ample for our needs. We had an outside cabin and an inside adjoining one— the outside cabin because Hazel can't sleep unless she's in a kind of slipstream of air, and the inside cabin because the kids had to be kept from crawling out of the portholes during the night in their eagerness to assure themselves they were really at sea.

Small as the cabins looked in the diagram, they were even smaller in reality. And what reduced their size even further was that all the baggage we had marked for the hold had been piled into the cabins. In plain fact we could not get into the cabins without climbing over a Himalaya of luggage. I was puzzled at the time about the reason why luggage plainly marked for storage during the voyage should have been dumped into our cabins. But the reason became plain later. None of the help spoke English.

It is curious that I had not thought of it before, but on a Greek ship people talk Greek. Some of the upper echelon, such as pursers, of course speak English. But pursers do not handle baggage, and Greek seamen cannot read labels written in English (though the printing on the labels was in plain English). And so all our bags were dumped in our tiny cabins and since there was no place to stand, we had all to take to the bunks and there we lay, wondering glumly whether this was to be our condition all the way across the Atlantic.

In the cabins themselves there was no place to stow any baggage. A suitcase or two could be squeezed under the lower berth but that was all. And there was a tiny hanging cupboard in which a man, with some ingenuity, might squeeze one suit, one frock for his wife, and perhaps a pair of pajamas. But this did little to remove the load, and matters were made that much worse by the fact that Tully, a dog of some sixty pounds, was in the cabin with us.

What to do?

During my days at school I had learned a fair amount of Greek but it was ancient Greek, and in the remnants which remained to me I could think of no phrase at all dealing with the removal of baggage to the hold or a bulldog to the kennels.

We rang the bell several times for the steward but without result, for the whole ship seemed to be in a similar state of confusion. I went to the purser's office and found a clamorous mob impassionately beseeching the purser's assistants (in Greek) to solve some critical problem for them without delay.

Finally I got the attention of an English-speaking purser and he agreed that the baggage would be removed and the dog would be taken out of our tiny cabin and kenneled. Then I went back to the cabins.

"All is solved," I said. "Let us go and have some lunch."

We went down to the dining room where there was an exotic taint of olive oil and garlic in the air.

I did not even look at the menu when the waiter handed it to me, for I knew what we wanted.

"Five servings of fried octopus," I said, "and some kind of baby food for Arabella. Also four glasses of milk. My wife and I will have coffee."

A look of panic came over the mobile features of the young Greek who waited on us.

"Cripes," I said to Hazel, "we're going to starve to death here. Nobody speaks English." What was the Greek word for octopus? How did one say "eight legs" in Greek? I tried counting in Greek but kept switching to French after four, or maybe it was Latin. Finally I wiggled my fingers at the steward and said "*pulpe*," which I vaguely recalled as being some kind of a Mediterranean word for an octopus. The steward retreated in terror.

He didn't come back for a while and meanwhile Hazel had taken the menu and looked it over. There was not a single familiar item on it. Another steward approached our table, for it seemed that the first was having hysterics in the kitchen. He said something in Greek. I bid him good day in English. He gave his name. I introduced the various members of our family. We all smiled at each other and a measure of international accord, though somewhat strained, was produced.

The steward swept some invisible crumbs off the table and produced a book and pencil. We stared glumly at the menu.

All the items on it were Grecian dishes. I started to wiggle my fingers again, for when I make up my mind about what I want to eat I am not to be readily diverted. Hazel stamped heavily on my foot under the table and smiled sweetly at the steward. When she smiles sweetly she has a radiant look like Katharine Hepburn discovering that the uneasy feelings from which she is suffering are not indigestion but love.

"*Leche,*" she said, "*por niños.*"

The steward wrote something on his pad.

"Since when do the Greeks talk Spanish?" I asked Hazel.

"Everybody speaks Spanish," she replied. She went on with the order, requesting "*comidas por bebe*" and pointing to an item on somebody else's table to indicate that we would have that instead of the fried octopus.

It's a pretty poor thing for a man to be shown up as a linguist by his wife, and I searched around for a phrase of French with which to impress the children.

"*Ouvrez la fenêtre, s'il vous plaît,*" I said, for that was all that came to my mind. The waiter wrote this down on his pad, too, smiled, bowed, and departed.

"What did you ask him, Daddy?" asked Kevin.

"I asked for fried octopus," I said, glowering at my wife.

What we got, when the waiter returned, was astonishing. There was a fish embalmed in spices and luxuriating in a bath of hot olive oil. This was followed by a kind of goulash in which we could not identify the meat. It seemed to have been cooked in Louisiana pepper sauce and was as hot as the doorknobs of hell. Hazel thought it was chicken and I thought it was lamb. The argument was purely academic because it tasted only of pepper. This was followed by ice cream for which we were grateful since we were as thirsty as if we had had a meal of burning coals. The children didn't get milk. They got coffee, and when finally I insisted in plain English and with some force on milk, a huge container of scalding hot milk was placed upon the table.

The steward then withdrew, presumably to inform his fellows that it had been his lot to draw a table full of madmen for the trip across the Atlantic.

We returned to the cabin burned, spiced, and garlicked. The baggage was still there and Tully still chained to the leg of the berth and panting pitifully in the heat.

This was the moment of complete demoralization.

Tricia climbed on top of the mound of bags in the children's cabin, sat down, and wept. Christopher demanded once more that he be taken back to Craigie's. I desperately needed some encouraging diversion to restore the spirits of all hands.

"Cheer up," I said. "At least we are going to get a brand-new car." I took out the ticket covering the passage on the automobile and for the first time noted that it said at the bottom "See Conditions on Back."

I turned the ticket over and discovered, in the ruby print, a horrifying clause which said that in case of damage to an automobile the company's liability was limited to one hundred dollars.

At that moment the ship's siren sounded, there was a kind of general shudder aboard the vessel, and I knew that we had cast off and were headed for Portugal.

The enormity of my sins were suddenly thrust upon me. I had sold my children's home, torn my family away from their dear friends, wrecked my car or put it in the hands of wreckers, put my children and my wife in a vessel bound for a completely unknown land (for us anyway), and not even provided them with decent accommodations aboard. And all because of reading the word "Portugal" on sardine cans in the supermarket.

Tully glowered at me and Hazel lay down silently in the berth and closed her eyes.

Kevin came over and patted my hand.

"Never mind, Daddy," he said, "we'll lick 'em yet."

He'll make a great president one day, that boy.

Life Among the Greeks

3.
FOR MYSELF, I AM A GREAT BE-
liever in the brotherhood of man and hold as barbarous anyone
who criticizes another because of race or nation. Despite these
liberal and humanitarian views it was soon borne in on me that
our present plight was owing to the fact that my family and I
were surrounded by blinking foreigners, and I proposed to do
something pretty stiff about it.

Accordingly I went once more to the purser's office to demand that Tully be taken to the dogs' quarters and was
urbanely assured that this would be done. Indeed the purser's
assistant called someone on the telephone and gave severe instructions in Greek, sufficient, I would think, to have kenneled all the dogs in New York.

But nothing happened.

It took three attempts before Tully was finally led off by a
seaman, and a little later I began to worry about what kind of
quarters had been allotted to him since ours were so crowded.
I found him on the topmost deck of the ship, in an open
kennel, shivering in the wind, and once more went to the
purser's office.

"Why is my dog exposed on the upper deck when we paid
his passage on the assurance that he would be in a sheltered
kennel?" I demanded.

The assistant assured me that the dog would shortly be removed to a special place for animals but in the present state of

chaos aboard ship this could not be done immediately. I checked a couple of times but Tully still yipped and shivered in the slipstream of the ship. Matters were no better in the cabins. The luggage was still piled high on the floor and no amount of demanding or cajoling was effective in getting the larger pieces removed to the hold. Ringing the bell for the steward was purely an exercise for the thumb, and Hazel needed a bottle of milk for Arabella but could not get it.

At last I went off to see the chief purser, that exalted dignitary who has even more control over the ship's passengers than the captain.

I found him in his office, a bald-headed man of massive features, with bold eyes and a heavy-set body. He sat at his desk and I, standing, had the uncomfortable feeling which must have overwhelmed Oliver Twist on that famous occasion when he asked for more.

"Our cabins are too small," I said, "and our luggage, even that which should be in the hold, is piled all over the floor. It is impossible for us to live in such quarters."

He looked up my name on the passenger list and considered his cabins. We had been assured by the travel agency that nothing larger could be obtained, but there must have been many cancellations, for several other cabins now offered.

"I can give you better quarters up forward," said the chief purser.

"Have you anything available in the first class?" I asked.

"It costs more in the first class," he replied.

"I am aware of that," I said stiffly, "but I do not want to travel tourist class on this ship." I trust I was giving the correct impression—that of perhaps a British resident magistrate making a protest to a foreign power. (Although Irish, I have lived long enough among the British to have noted those tones of voice which they used, in the past, to run matters around the world.)

"You have money?" asked the purser, so apparently I had failed as a British resident magistrate, for such a question would never be put to so austere a personage.

"Of course," I replied, taking out my wallet which was positively bulging with ten-dollar bills—the remnants of my bank account in the United States after payment of fares and income tax.

The wallet did the trick.

"Sit down," said the chief purser. "Service is much better in the first class. Have a cigarette." He produced a silver case. It was just like turning on an electric light. I was transformed from Oliver Twist into the beadle himself in a moment.

The purser now seemed entirely on our side, intimating, though without a word spoken, that he had known all along that we were first-class personages, quite out of their element in the tourist class, though it was hardly his place to say so.

He seemed pleased that we should, on our own, have found our right level and called the captain to request formal permission for us to move from tourist to the upper decks.

More than that, he proposed to the captain that he discount the additional price by 40 per cent, and so rendered me a signal service, for had I booked the first-class berths ashore, they would have cost an additional one hundred and sixty dollars.

All that before had been vexing was now charming. Our luggage was whisked by first-class stewards out of the tourist-class depths and we were placed in cabins with beds instead of bunks, with a chair to sit in (a chair could by no means have been placed in the other cabins), and a dressing table at which Hazel could make up plus closets in which clothes could be hung.

Our steward introduced himself as Johannes with good humor and dignity, and proved a man of sufficient character to reprimand Christopher for getting on one of the beds with his shoes on, so that I liked and respected him immediately.

He told us the time for dinner, bustled off to get a bottle of milk for Arabella as if this was service which gave him pleasure, assisted with the unpacking of our clothes, and laid out a good suit for me while I was in the shower.

What a delightful thing money is! [I rarely have it in any large quantity so I am not used to the blessings it can buy.] I will not say a harsh word against it for the rest of my life.

Even Tully benefited from the change, for when, bathed and clad in a clean suit, and my beard combed, I went to see how he fared, I found that he had been taken to quite wonderful quarters, sheltered from the wind, and with several other dogs and a couple of guinea hens as company.

He, too, it seemed, was now to go first class.

That night at dinner we found a menu such as one might find in any better-class restaurant, and although it did not feature fried octopus, and I was never to sample that dish, it did feature such essentials as chops and steaks and scallops of veal and Dover sole grilled in butter, which is the only proper anointment for the Dover sole when dead.

All went forward now most pleasantly as far as quarters and service were concerned.

"One should never travel anywhere except first class," I told Hazel over an after-dinner cigar. "On the other hand," I reflected soberly, "we have only nine dollars and sixty cents between us."

But Hazel refused to be ruffled. That first-class feeling, that all is well in the world, had taken hold of her firmly.

"Cable Mary for some money," she said. Mary is my literary agent in New York.

"But we have all the money Mary had for us," I replied, wondering what the purser would say if I went back to him to say we didn't like the first-class quarters and wished to be transferred to the tourist once more and would like our money refunded.

"Mary will send you some money," said Hazel, who has enormous faith in her.

But I did not like the idea and began to suspect that I was not after all a first-class personage, but was masquerading and would shortly be exposed. The stewards no longer looked so

friendly and polite, and I developed a positive dread of the
purser.

In the end I went to the ship's bank and asked casually
whether I might cash a check on my Lisbon bank where I
had transferred what money I could to live on in Portugal.

I was told, by no means casually, that I could not. I walked
around the deck and looked into the first-class passengers'
lounge, but it was quiet and opulent and at that moment
seemed to scorn me. In the end I went to the radio room and
sent a message to Mary which read "Car wrecked. Can you
send one hundred dollars?" Whatever the effect in New York
of this startling message, the money arrived within a few
hours. To steady my nerves, I let it lie in the ship's bank for
two days, until I had had several messages asking that I call
for it. To such extremes are mice driven in their anxiety to
achieve the status of men.

As part of being first-class people we were invited to dine
with the captain. It was altogether a doleful dinner because
we could find no topic of conversation of mutual interest. The
children were fed first, in the cabin, by Johannes, who seemed
to take to himself some of the glory of having his temporary
master and mistress invited to the captain's table. I fancy he
gave an especially hard look at my tie as I left for the dinner
to assure himself that it did credit not so much to me as to
him. The children's dinner out of the way, we went down to
the dining room to be escorted to the captain's table.

"Your children have eaten already?" the captain said
anxiously, and when we replied that they had, he seemed re-
lieved. I could not blame him. It would be an ordeal for any
man to dine with four children, all strange to him.

We sat down, and since I had determined to avoid the
obvious question, "How long have you been at sea, Captain?"

there was a moment's guarded hiatus of communication. The captain could have, had he wished, inquired after the children. But he was a veteran, no doubt, of many dinners with passengers and had learned not to bring up the subject of their children. I do the same thing myself. And I, sure that the unfortunate man was tired to death of being asked how many years he had been at sea, said nothing on that score.

We found a little mutual territory in the fact that I had yoghurt with my dinner and so did the captain. The captain said the Mediterranean peoples eat yoghurt because it is good for them. I then started to discuss the reasons why *I* eat yoghurt.

The reasons why I eat yoghurt are very interesting but they become involved because there is a long story to my yoghurt.

It started with tennis, and that's the only bright thing about it. One day I was playing tennis with my wife and she beat me six love, six love, six love, and then I got fed up and as my mind obviously wasn't on tennis and I could beat her easily if it was, I said I ought to go in and write on a book.

So I went back to my study and opened the window and my wife went shopping. I had been working away on the book for about an hour when it occurred to me that I ought to get up and look out the window in case there were any ideas outside. And when I stood up my whole upper torso was drenched with pain. Buckets of agony flowed down my arms and I had as hard a time fetching my breath as if someone had put an anvil on my chest. Plainly I was about to die of a massive heart attack, and I felt pretty mad about it because I knew that Hazel was trying on hats in the hour of my death, Amen.

I dragged myself down to the car, got in, started it, and drove down to the doctor. I had a strep throat on top of everything else but I have strep throats so often I hardly even bother to mention them.

It took a little while to see the doctor because there were apparently several other people dying ahead of me. When I saw him, he made me open my mouth and then informed me I had a strep throat which I had told him in the first place. He said the strep throat had gone to my arms and that was why they hurt so much. He then gave me four billion units of penicillin in the buttock and I drove home and crawled into bed.

When Hazel came back with a new hat I told her I was dying and to call another doctor. She called one who came and asked me how I felt. I said I was moribund, and he sat down on the bed with a hearty laugh and told me I had a strep throat after I opened my mouth.

I was a little weary of arguing about it by then, and asked for some kind of painkiller as my chest and arms hurt so much. This he prescribed.

A couple of days later I felt pretty good and got up, but I still had a strep throat.

So I went back to the doctor and what with one thing and another he thought I might have had a heart attack and sent me for an electrocardiogram. The electrocardiogram reported that I was suffering from a heart block; the timing mechanism of the upper part of the heart was out of whack with the pumping mechanism in the lower part of the heart. If I stopped smoking I might live long enough to finish the book.

But I still had the strep throat.

So I went to another doctor and told him that I knew I had a bad heart but could he cure my strep throat? He doubted I had a bad heart and hooked me up to the city electric supply again and came back with a report that my heart was as sound as a brass-bound boiler.

He took a swab of my throat and said I had a chronic strep throat but he'd fix it. He gave me some medicine that cost about five dollars per cyedropper full and told me more or less to take it every three hours until I couldn't feel a thing.

And that's where the yoghurt came in. Because between the billion units of penicillin and the concentrated doses of aureomycin or streptomycin or whatever it was, the strep throat was cured but all the little bugs necessary to digestion were killed off in a general massacre. In short, I couldn't digest anything—nothing at all.

And then another doctor said that I ought to eat yoghurt. So I ate yoghurt for six solid months and gradually I restocked my insides with the necessary bugs and began to take a little nourishment.

I maintain that, taking in the tennis and everything, the reasons why I eat yoghurt are very interesting indeed, but when I had got through with the recital, the captain was looking dull-eyed at the table, and Hazel was getting impatient because she was waiting to tell the captain why *she* drinks buttermilk.

I could see, in short, that the captain wasn't interested in my yoghurt and cast around for some other topic with which to cheer him up.

For many years I have been the sea serpent editor of the *Rocky Mountain Herald*—a newspaper which, scorning the mere gossip that passes for news these days, has collaborated with me in launching a worldwide search for sea serpents and also has an editor in charge of mice, and another in charge of signs of the times (outdoor advertising), and so on. Now one of my jobs as sea serpent editor of the *Rocky Mountain*

Herald is to try to contact people who have seen, or think they have seen, sea serpents. The captain, I knew, had been long at sea, and so was a likely prospect.

"Captain," I said, "have you ever seen a sea serpent?"

A look almost of fright came into his eyes. I think he had come to the conclusion that not only had he a lunatic on board but he was dining with him at the moment.

"No," he said. "I have never seen a sea serpent."

He then called the steward and said something to him in Greek, and the steward went away and came back and announced in English that the captain was wanted on the bridge.

"I wish you wouldn't keep asking people about sea serpents," Hazel said, who was vexed, as I say, because she hadn't got around to her buttermilk.

"It's better than talking to them about how we're all going to be blown up tomorrow or die of bone cancer," I replied, and I fancy I scored there.

Anyway, it was a pretty dull dinner with the captain, and when we were later invited to the captain's cocktail party for the whole ship, he saw to it that we were seated with a gentleman who had the most tedious tale to tell about some accident or other in which he had put his knee out of joint. A pretty dirty trick, in my view.

Actually the most interesting person on board proved to be the chief purser. He took to inviting me to his office in the latter part of the afternoon for a drink, and we talked on all manner of subjects. One day we discussed violins and how strange it was that although many of the great instruments of Stradivarius, Guarnerius, Rogeri, Amati, and Breganza had been copied in microscopic detail, the copies were not a patch on the original instrument.

"It is pretty generally accepted that the secret does not lie in the varnish either," I said. "Actually we have finer varnishes today than were available in the seventeenth century."

"Of course it has nothing to do with the varnish," said the purser. "It has to do with life—the life force of the man who made the original and which still exists in the instrument long after we say the man is dead. The imitation instruments sound like copies because they are made by people who were copying and not creating. When a man makes an original piece of work, he puts a part of himself into it. That can never be copied."

While I was talking with the purser in the evenings the children would be in the lounge of the ship playing bingo with the other passengers. One day Kevin won four dollars and fifty cents. He was so happy he kept jumping up and down in his bunk crying, "I won. I won. Everybody was there and saw and they know that I won. Hurray. Hurray," and he thumped his pillow with soaring, uncontrolled joy.

Hazel told me everyone in the lounge was delighted that Kevin had won. The captain kissed him, and Patricia and Christopher were so happy they kissed the captain. There was a great deal of kissing all around.

It took a long time to get the children to sleep that night. Kevin slept with his four dollars and fifty cents under his pillow. Christopher had his good old rubber hunting knife under his—in case of attack by sea rovers or pirates or captains sailing under letters of mart or counter mart, I suppose.

For myself, I lost constantly at bingo, and had to borrow Kevin's four dollars and fifty cents. I suppose this was reprehensible behavior, but I consoled myself (though not Kevin) with the thought that I was giving him a lesson in the futility of gambling.

4.

BEFORE SETTING OUT ON OUR
journey we had made some inquiries about living costs in
Portugal and had received a wonderful variety of replies to
these. Various magazine articles stated that one might live like
a Vanderbilt in Portugal on an income amounting to a hundred
dollars a month. One could eat a surfeit of shrimp and lobster
in excellent restaurants for a dollar a head, and five dollars
would serve for an evening on the town in Lisbon.

The Portuguese consulate in New York reported that I
would be able to rent an unfurnished six-room apartment in
Lisbon for forty dollars a month. His confrere in Los Angeles
said I could have a house for fifty dollars a month.

But when I called on the Portuguese information service in
New York prior to sailing, I was told that a house would cost
me two hundred dollars a month, and a moment of panic set
in. A Portuguese official traveling on the ship informed me that
a good house could be rented outside Lisbon for a hundred
dollars a month. The scale, then, ranged from forty dollars a
month to two hundred dollars a month with no sure sounding
anywhere.

Some whom I consulted proclaimed Portugal one of the
cheapest countries in Europe and others announced that it
was almost as expensive as France; a country so expensive that
not even Americans can afford it. Guidebooks were no help.
Guidebooks are basically for tourists and so give no firm indi-

cation of living costs but only tourist costs. Nobody on board had ever lived in Portugal and most of them, being Greek, were horrified at the thought of doing so. We learned that swarms of Portuguese beggars pounced on every passenger who landed at Lisbon and haggled with him for his baggage. The ship's entertainment officer each afternoon showed slides of the various countries which the ship touched at.

Those of Greece were beautiful, all flowers and mountains and sunsets and purple seas.

Those of Portugal were miserable. Every picture seemed to have been taken in the midst of a rainstorm. The trees were bare, the gardens of the houses bedraggled, and the few specimens of architecture depicted looked like those gingerbread ornaments once a favorite tenant of Edwardian mantelpieces.

In short, the nearer we came to Portugal, the more the lure of the place receded. I had fancied living in a villa in some small fishing village, with a view of the sea and the fishing boats, and with brown fishermen and their buxom wives as our neighbors. But it seemed that we were more likely to be living in a rain-swept city populated by beggars and with a thousand smells, all obnoxious, constantly in our nostrils.

We arrived off Lisbon in the heart of a November gale. A murky night, thick with wind and rain, enveloped the ship, and we lay outside the mouth of the Tagus, in this witches' brew of weather, for some several hours, awaiting the arrival of the pilot boat. This came at last, visible only as a mast light that bobbed and plunged in the heavy seas. The pilot got aboard and with his aid the ship groped forward out of the foul Atlantic into the mouth of the Tagus where the water was quieter but the rain sluiced down in sheets behind a merciless wind.

I had always thought of Portugal as a land drenched in

sunlight, but its prospect now was no more inviting than Manchester in an evil mood. Of the city itself we could see only a few lights strong enough to penetrate the wildness of the night.

Somewhere ashore there was a huge and grim building, like a leftover army barracks, and this we knew was the customs shed where we would soon be standing getting clearance for our baggage.

A ferry or two crossed the river, attesting to the seamanship of the Portuguese, for the river was a cauldron. And the captain of our vessel, in view of the ferocity of the night, had decided that to attempt to dock the ship would be inviting a wreck. We learned through the grapevine that we were to anchor in midstream and all of us would go ashore in lighters, soaking wet, of course, and with our baggage in similar condition.

This brought a reaction close to mutinous from the passengers. They pronounced the captain lily-livered, incompetent, derelict in his duty, and seemed on the verge of begging the first mate to take over.

An extremely long conference on whether to dock or unload with the use of lighters seemed to be taking place, for we remained in midstream for two hours, and finally tugs were summoned which impertinently warped the big ship over to the dock and we tumbled out of it like bees from an overturned hive—bags, dogs, passengers, stewards, porters, ship's officials, and children—plunging ashore in a swarm of excitement.

It was now after ten at night and I anticipated that what with clearing our bags and getting the necessary clearance for Tully we might easily be in the custom's shed for a further two hours.

But now we met, for the first time, that courtesy which is characteristic of the Portuguese. The porters, far from being a haggling, begging horde, helped sort our baggage efficiently, inquired which bags we needed immediately, and got these taken to the customs inspectors with a minimum of fuss. All this was achieved by pantomime, for the porter who adopted us could not speak English and I had no knowledge of Portuguese. I carried on an astonishing conversation in French with the health officer to get Tully cleared—astonishing in that I discovered that I knew some French. In quite a short time, then, we were through, and had taken a taxi to a hotel recommended by the Portuguese official who had traveled with the ship.

The frontage of this establishment would have done credit to the Waldorf-Astoria. There was a magnificent flight of snowy marble steps leading up to clean-cut glass-and-chromium doors. The lobby was an extensive prairie of soft carpet with here and there a graceful palm and a nest of modern chairs holding a conversation around a low coffee table. I had soon booked a suite of rooms and had been informed that the dog could spend the night in the bathroom. Portugal, despite the foulness of the night, began to take on some of its old allure.

But the allure did not last long.

We were conducted to a wing of the hotel where all the splendor of the lounge immediately vanished. Now, instead of luxurious carpets, there were threadbare mats; instead of walls elegantly paneled, there were walls papered in dreary brown paper; instead of marble stairs, there were wooden stairs which creaked their age under our weight.

The rooms allotted us were large but smelled of wet leather or perhaps it was wet flannel. Or maybe it was wet wallpaper.

The beds were of the kind which have wrought-iron head-
boards and footboards and the mattresses were thin and stuffed
with raw cotton which had collected in huddles in various
parts, humping its back, as it were, to get out of the omni-
present damp. There was a washstand in each room with two
very tiny taps, one labeled *"fria"* and the other *"quente."*
They both gave "fria" water. In short, the suite of rooms had
all the charm of a place closed in mourning on the death of
Queen Victoria and only opened again to welcome the arrival
of the Wibberleys, and that without any airing.

We got the children gloomily to bed and put Tully in the
bathroom and then went to our own room. There were big
French windows with folding shutters which cut the rooms off
from a tiny wrought-iron balcony outside. We undressed, and
the dampness laid its clammy fingers on our flesh as we did so.

"I'm afraid the children will get pneumonia," said Hazel.

I coughed, and it sounded to me like the cough of a man
whose lungs had finally fallen into tatters. We had had a nice
comfortable home in southern California. The sun had shone
most of the time and we used to go down on the beach in
November and lie there until it was too hot and then race into
the exhilarating chill of the sea. In our home in California we
had had floor furnaces and a big fireplace in which I burned
orangewood logs. Everything was always dry there.

I tried to think of something positive and cheerful to say. I
looked at our bed and said, "There are plenty of blankets,
thank God."

So there were. Lots of them. We crawled in and lay still,
looking up at the ceiling. The ceiling had been painted, probably during the rebuilding of Lisbon after the earthquake, and
all the colors had faded. There was a combination of geometrical and floral designs woven together with astoundingly

bad taste. Lying on our backs it was as if we were looking at a huge, colored anatomical drawing, showing the muscles, liver, spleen, and other unpleasant parts of a cadaver.

Still it was interesting in an intensely morbid and depressing way.

"It's a pity the taste for painted ceilings has gone out of fashion," I said. "Ceiling paintings produced some of the world's greatest art treasures, as witness the Vatican ceiling painted by Michelangelo."

"The bed's damp," said Hazel.

So it was. It was more than damp. It was moist. The mattress sagged heavily toward the center of the bed, and lying in it was like lying in a bog. I sniffed and felt the covers. They were damp, too. The floors were damp and the walls were damp and the ceiling was damp and the bed was damp and so was I and so was Hazel.

"The hell with it," I said, "let's go out somewhere cheerful and have a dish of those huge scarlet shrimps we saw in that magazine article."

We dressed and peeked at the kids, who seemed to be steaming a little in their damp beds, and hailed a taxi. The taxi driver spoke only Portuguese and so we went through all the elaborate pantomime of telling him to take us to a restaurant. He succeeded brilliantly, taking us to a restaurant in the Rossio or older part of Lisbon which would have done credit to the best that Beverly Hills could offer.

One wall was occupied by an enormous picture in painted tiles of a submarine scene. The gradation of colors was beautiful and moving. One could feel the green, clean wetness of the ocean water. Seaweed and fish floated across these painted tiles in liquid grace. Every kind of sea creature of the smaller size was shown—schools of tiny perch and fierce old crabs and big cod and so on. The Portuguese are at their best when dealing in sea subjects and here none can touch them.

In the center of the restaurant was a huge illuminated tank of fish—big fish floating silently around in pale green water with silver bubbles, like jewels, rising around them. To one side was a large fountain, again with a sea motif, and its merry splashing was the most graceful sound in all the world.

Suddenly the damp beds and the miserable hotel rooms didn't matter. We smiled at each other. Here was the Portugal we wanted to see—the Portugal that loved the sea and whose essence was of the sea. The whole place was different and enchanting, a work both of love and of artistry.

Hazel sighed contentedly.

"I wonder what the Portuguese word for 'shrimps' is," she said.

I reached back into my schoolboy Latin—something I was to do increasingly in my struggle to gain a working knowledge of Portuguese. Cancer was crab. But what was shrimp? Where in "De Gallico Bello" or the verses of Ovid had there been any reference made to shrimps?

Nowhere.

The waiter stood politely by and finally I looked around and saw a man with a plateful of scarlet shrimps before him.

"Gusto," I said, pointing.

The waiter went away and returned with a huge tray of them. They were delicious. We ate in happy enjoyment, conscious that we had arrived in fairyland even though the beds were damp there.

"Tomorrow I'll find you a house," I told Hazel. "I'll get one on a mountain with a big garden and a floor furnace."

"And there'll be a cook who looks like a gipsy and wears big golden earrings," Hazel said.

"Where did you get that from?" I asked.

"I just know," said Hazel.

And by golly she was right.

5.

IN ALL OUR TIME IN PORTUGAL
I never did discover what Portuguese children take for their
breakfast. Whatever they drink at breakfast time, it is certainly not milk, for milk seems to be regarded in Portugal
with that horror which in the American Midwest is accorded
to wine.

On the day after our arrival I ordered breakfast to be served
in our rooms. I ordered it in a mixture of French, English, and
Portuguese taken out of a guidebook which I held on my
knee. I asked for brioches, café, and *"leite quente por niños,"*
and what I got was mounds of hard toasted rolls, pots of hot
and navy-strong coffee, and jugs of scalding milk which would
have melted lips of brass.

This was brought in by a waiter who hovered around, not
for a tip, but to see what in the name of goodness we were
going to do with this collection. We put all the jugs of milk in
the hand basin, to his astonishment, and filled the hand basin
with cold water. We poured coffee for ourselves, and he,
hoping to be helpful, poured coffee for the children—the kind
of coffee that drove men mad at sea.

We shooed the waiter out of the room and tried to fill a
bottle of boiling hot milk for Arabella. But the milk had a skin
on it and kept clogging the nipple and I could see ahead of us
a wearying struggle with nipples and the skin of boiled milk.

I tried to get a strainer, but if there is a Portuguese word for such an articles, it is not listed in the dictionaries.

I remember reading in my childhood how men stricken with thirst in the Brazilian jungles had strained green water through fine linen handkerchiefs which they happened to have with them. I found a fine linen handkerchief, and cheered on by Kevin, who has enormous faith in me, tried to strain the milk through it.

But the milk floated around in a horrid bulge in the handkerchief and then overflowed on the floor, so I was left with a handkerchief sodden with milk, milk on the floor, and Arabella crying. Furthermore, I scalded my hand. I flung the handkerchief out of the window and announced that I was going down to the bank to get some money and that I would get a taxi and we would look for a house, and for goodness' sakes have the children ready when I got back. (I have found that when I have made a mess of things around the house, the only way to recover face is to give a few orders and get out. This is cowardice, of course, but every man to his own defenses.)

Out I went then, down to the bank where I got some money with remarkable ease and came back. And in the interim Hazel had washed all the children, clothed them, and washed out a large number of diapers; fed everybody and got herself dressed and hung up a lot of the clothing so that I knew (and not for the first time) that I had certainly married a kind of domestic genius. The damp room was now strewn with damp diapers, and the whole place was as unhealthy as a t.b. ward.

Then we got a taxi to go house hunting. The taxi driver's name was Texeira, which is roughly pronounced Tayshera. He spoke a word or two of English. He could say "Good

day" and "Where to?" But since I did not know where to
myself, this did not help very much.

I got hold of one of the hotel staff who spoke English and
asked him to tell the taxi driver that we wished to rent a house
near the sea and outside of Lisbon. "Not in Estoril," I said, for
Estoril is the place where European kings go when they have
lost their jobs, and most of them seem to have taken the
treasury with them, for they have a lot of money. We couldn't
then afford a house in so high-priced an area.

"Estoril," said the hotel man to Texeira.

Whether we wished it or not we were going to be a
neighbor of former kings.

There is a fine road leading from the heart of Lisbon out to
Estoril. It is a four-lane divided highway and is called the
Auto-Strada.

We had then, on our first morning, an excellent view of
Lisbon, for I had managed to convey to Texeira that we
wished to take our dog to some place where he could be kenneled. The Portuguese have, in the Lisbon zoo, a special area
in which dogs are boarded which is called the "Hotel of
Dogs," and in driving there we saw much of the city.

To drive around Lisbon is to experience the adventure of
an ant which is crawling around in the frosting of a wedding
cake. The city is replete with statuary which is all white and
highly ornamental. The houses are also ornamental, for the
Portuguese, in making anything at all, contrive to make it not
only useful but pretty. They take a childlike and enchanting
delight in decoration for the sake of decoration. We passed
blocks of houses with beautiful wrought-iron balconies outside each window and with the whole façade covered with
colored tiles. Some of these tiles were in heavenly blues or
crisp greens, and with the white of other buildings close by,

and the whole structure capped with a red roof, are joyous
to behold. Some of the tiles, however, were a horrid brown
and in the worst of taste. They were jarring to the eye, and
the longer we stayed in Portugal the more we became aware
of how excellent taste and abominable taste are intermingled
in the Portuguese nature.

But to return to the statues. It seems that no event in Portuguese history is left without its monument. Thus there was a
statue to mark the restoration of the monarchy and not far
away a statue to mark the overthrow of the monarchy and the
founding of the republic. There are statues to kings and to
those who overthrew kings, and all these statues, with their
pedestals gushing wreaths of flowers and vines, could never,
after the first glance, be mistaken for anything but Portuguese.

White and elaborate, found in every square or in the center
of every main street, they give a wedding-cake air to the city.

Lisbon is built upon a series of hills, steep, impetuous hills
that rush up and down like the waves of the ocean, carrying
their rows of decorated houses on their sides. The city has a
certain joyousness and exhilaration and cleanliness which re-
minded me of the great ocean waves, far from the land, with
the wind flinging over them and the air around sparkling with
sunlit spray. In building Lisbon the Portuguese have built, perhaps not unwittingly, a vast monument to the ocean, with
which they have been in love through all their history and of
which they were once the acknowledged masters.

There are those who will say that a city reminiscent of a
wedding cake could hardly be described at the same time as a
monument to the majesty and exhilaration of the ocean. But
these are the sort who have never minutely examined either

the ocean or the sweeping decorations of wedding cakes, for on a brisk day at sea there is much in common between the two.

We bowled out of Lisbon toward Estoril on the Auto-Strada, plunging, in the city's environs, up hills which find their only American counterpart in San Francisco, and finally came to the ocean. Here Hazel made one of her more unfortunate remarks of the trip.

Looking at the ocean, the sand, the boulevard flanking the beach, and the bouquets of houses on the landward side, Spanish-tiled, with hibiscus and palms in the garden, and red geraniums sprouting from every semi-cultivated point, she said,

"It looks like California."

"Woman," I said, "I have sold our home, wrecked our car, spent nearly two thousand dollars on fares one way and another, and disposed of most of our possessions to get you here. I do not wish to be told that it looks exactly like the place we left. Look at the differences. Look at the tiles on those houses there—blue splashes of daring color against the sun-parched wall." (The wall actually was streaming with rain, as was everything else.)

"I'm sick of tiles," said Hazel. "Besides, they make tiles in California."

"Look, then, at the upturned corners of the roofs of the houses—turned upward as a mark that the Portuguese were the first to establish a colony in the Celestial Land of China."

Hazel looked and said nothing.

"They're like those old kinds of houses they had in Los Angeles before they put in the freeways, aren't they, Daddy?" said Kevin, who at times is achingly devoid of tact. I gave up

and turned to Texeira, anxious to be sure that he understood
we were looking for a house to rent among fishermen and not
among the former kings. But I could find no pantomime to
express the words former king and attempts to assure him that
I was but a poor working author did nothing. He compre-
hended only that I was an author, and since it is basic that any
man who gets a book published is rich, he was bound on taking
me to the most expensive neighborhood around Lisbon.

When we got to Estoril I inquired at the tourist bureau
where we might rent a house and was directed to a real-estate
agency nearby. A charming lady rose to greet me.

"*A Senhora fala Inglis?*" I asked, having rehearsed this sentence all the way from Lisbon.

"Yes," she said with a smile. "What can I do for you?"

I knew I had found a friend, and with a word to St. Patrick
not to desert me now in foreign parts, I announced that I was
the father of four children and was looking for a furnished
house nearby.

"I have such a house," said the lady. "It is not in Estoril but
in a village nearby—Malveira da Serra. It has three bedrooms,
a large living room, servants' quarters, and the usual facilities,
and about two acres of ground. There is also central heating
and hot water."

"And the rent?"

"Three thousand escudos a month. [About one hundred and
twenty dollars.] You may have it on a lease until April. After
that the owner will be returning. Your children . . .?" She did
not finish the sentence but I knew what she intended.

"They are young," I said. "The eldest is not yet eight, the
youngest, eighteen months. They are also civilized and accustomed to living in houses."

We looked at each other candidly for a few seconds and she smiled. "I think they will be all right," she said. "Here, I will give you the key and send a man with you and you can look the house over and see if it suits you."

I returned to Hazel. "I have found us a house," I said. "Three bedrooms, living room, central heating, hot water, large garden, servants' quarters, and so on."

Hazel was a little taken aback. I have never failed to provide her with a house, but the ease with which I find them always surprises her.

"Servants?" she said, as only a young American girl can say the word—with excitement and a tinge of fear, perhaps awe.

"Yes, there is a girl who lives at the house and does the cooking and light cleaning. Her husband is with her. But he works elsewhere. Built-in baby sitters if nothing else."

"I'll bet she has gold earrings," said Hazel.

We drove in silence out to the house. It seemed an infinitely long way, halfway up a mountain and over some lonely strips of moorland and through two tiny villages. The moorland looked desolate and the rain pelted down on it with mournful intensity. Up and up we climbed and still could get no glimpse of the house. And then we turned into a muddy road leading through a spur of pine forest and found before us an iron gateway with an acacia draped over it. The gateway was open and we drove up a driveway through a garden planted with fruit trees, geraniums, and bright patches of chrysanthemums. The house was perched above the garden on a slab of lawn. I noted a huge glass frontage to the living room and thought of California, and then the door was opened before we even had time to look for the key.

Before us stood a dark-haired, swarthy, pretty Portuguese

woman in her late twenties. She had a smile like a dentifrice
advertisement and a look between deference and mischief in
her dark-brown eyes.

And suspended from her ear lobes were large gold earrings.
I knew that we had found our Portuguese home.

6.

THE GIRL WHO HAD ANSWERED
the door was named Maria and she was the cook.

I have said that her complexion was swarthy but some quali-
fication of this statement is needed. When she was happy, her
face was snuff brown but her cheeks showed a delicate rose
pink. Her teeth sparkled and her eyes sparkled and even her
hair seemed to sparkle.

But when she was sad, she was somber. She drooped. A
smoldering rebellion emerged from her and she had a way of
going about so quietly and resentfully that it would have been
better if she had clattered the dishes and slammed the doors to
vent her grievances.

Her husband's name was Marco. He was seven or eight
years younger than Maria and she adored him and lived in
constant dread that she might, in one way or another, lose his
affections.

So that while Maria served us, and did so well, all things
considered, her major concern was not to offend her handsome young husband; not in any way to risk a lessening of his
love for her. Thus we were, in a sense, a means of helping
Maria to keep the affections of Marco, though we did not
realize this for some time.

The household staff also included a gardener, Tomaso, and
his wife, Celita. Tomaso was as shy as a boy and painfully

anxious to please. He was slight of build and wore clothes two sizes too big for him. Whenever he caught sight of me, he would stop whatever he was doing and give me a bow from the waist, at the same time removing the little black beret which he wore at all times.

I used to write in the living room before the huge sliding glass doors with which it was equipped. From here I had a view of the lawn before the house, the village of Malveira da Serra below, then the moorlands and hills with tiny windmills atop them, and far in the distance the mouth of the Tagus where it meets the Atlantic Ocean.

It was necessary for Tomaso to pass this window many times a day during his work in the garden. He would always stop square in front of me, give me his bow, and remove his beret. I, in return, would nod my head and smile. We liked each other immediately, I fancy.

Yet such courtesies can play hob with literary production, and eventually I had to give up my lovely view and write facing a wall of the living room so as not to be interrupted in mid-inspiration by the bowing Tomaso.

Celita, Tomaso's wife, was as massive as he was slim. She looked like an Epstein statue come to life. Her limbs were big and her head was big and her body was big and her lips were big and her nose was big.

Her heart was big, too.

She was clumsy and at times lazy, and one would have thought that so huge a body could hardly have contained much fire of spirit. And yet Celita was quite as fiery as the slimmer and prettier Maria. Sometimes the two quarreled. Maria regarded herself, being the resident domestic, as the housekeeper and head of all the others. She would issue her orders sharply, not in the considerate way of the non-Latin, but in a peremptory manner. Sometimes Celita would sulk a little. Sometimes she would erupt and from the kitchen would come a crossfire of high-pitched Portuguese while we sat in the living room pretending all was serene.

Then the combatants would realize how much noise they were making and there would be an instant quiet, full of repentance. And then, to make amends, Maria would come in and say,

"*Cha por senhor?*"

Tea was her invariable peace offering, and one which I never refused.

It did not take us long to realize that of all our domestic staff Maria was the one to be dealt with and dealt with firmly. I suppose it is true that all domestics will seek to obtain the upper hand of their employers and so a struggle for control

must be firmly and politely waged until the master or mistress
has either finally demonstrated authority or has lost his or her
position as head of the household.

The contest, quiet but firm, between ourselves and Maria
was soon joined. We did not immediately move into our house,
but gave her two days in which to get matters in order for us,
and told her we would arrive in time for dinner on the third
day. I did this through an interpreter from the real-estate office,
for Maria spoke no English and was firm in her determination
to learn none.

But when we arrived on the third day there was no food in
the house and no *jantar* (dinner) had been prepared. Maria
told us this calmly, awaiting our reaction, testing us out. She
suggested that we return to Cascais (for food was not to be
purchased in Malveira da Serra) and eat our dinner there.

But I suspected that it would be wrong to capitulate in this
manner. I went to Cascais, bought bacon, eggs, bread, milk,
coffee, and other necessities, and returned with them.

I took them into the kitchen and we opened the parcels.
Maria exclaimed over the bacon, as if she had never seen such
strange produce before. She made it quite clear that she did
not know how to cook bacon, but I was ready for this.

I found a frying pan, lit the small gas stove with which the
kitchen was equipped, and put on the bacon. Then in exe-
crable Portuguese I told Maria that in America we had no
servants, we had got along splendidly without them, and that
I, although a senhor and an author, could cook any kind of
meal.

Maria summoned Tomaso and Marco and Celita to enjoy
the spectacle of the Senhor cooking dinner in the kitchen.
Meanwhile, I told Kevin to find some plates and cups and lay

the table which was in the living room. Kevin did so. Maria saw herself in some danger. This strange American family could seemingly shift for itself. Where did that leave her? Did it not make her to some extent unnecessary?

Suddenly she turned to Celita and issued a stream of orders. And Celita bustled into the living room and put on a tablecloth and took the cutlery and dishes from Kevin and laid the table for us.

Nothing had been done, despite the two days' notice, about warming the house. Portugal in winter has days of cold driving rain, and the house had a feeling of interior wetness and all was frigid.

"*Onde ligne por fugo?*" I asked, for I had been giving myself a blitz course in Portuguese—or at least those words and phrases of Portuguese having to do with domestic needs.

The four looked at each other. And then Tomaso smiled. He bowed, and since inside our house he always took off his beret, he now swept the floor with it in a gesture which would have brought a nod of approval from Sir Walter Raleigh. It was raining but he plunged outside and returned with an armful of logs and soon had a good fire going in the living room.

I put a hand on the radiator.

"*Fria,*" I said.

"*Si, senhor,*" said Tomaso.

"*Noa gusto fria,*" I replied.

"*Si, senhor,*" said Tomaso, and off he went to light the furnace and get some heat through the pipes.

We were making some progress, asserting a necessary authority; showing that we expected things to be done. But Maria still had some reservations.

She wanted to find out a few important matters about us, and the most important was our estate in life.

Had we much money?

That was critical to Maria, affecting, as it did, her own status in the world of domestics. When she went to market she must be able to mention, quite casually to all from whom she bought food, that her employer had *muito dinheiro*.

The first thing to be settled was whether we had an automobile. An automobile is an essential mark of rank in Portugal. In older times, horsemen, *cabalheiros*, were gentlemen and those who walked afoot, peasants. Now car owners are the cabalheiros and the foot people are still peasants.

Portuguese civil servants, however miserable their salaries, have cars. And they have chauffeurs for their cars, for no man of any mark with great problems of state on his mind can be expected to concern himself with driving a car to and from work. Thus clerks in government ministries sit in the back of Volkswagens and Fiats, their knees almost jammed into the back of the chauffeur up front who is driving them.

Maria then inquired if Senhor Leonard had an automobile, and I attempted to explain that my car had been dropped from a crane while being loaded in New York. This was a difficult enough matter to explain in English and quite beyond my powers in Portuguese. I did not know the word for automobile and, trying a shot in the dark, used the word *caro*. This brought a giggle from Celita, for it seemed that I was confessing a certain tender regard for Maria. I tried again in some confusion, but I did not believe that in this first effort to explain about our car I achieved anything.

Maria then explained that her husband, Marco, had a beautiful bicycle but that it had been wrecked in an automobile accident and Marco had had to spend some days in hospital. His splendid bicycle was all smashed up and would cost a great deal of money to fix.

She seemed infinitely sad as she related this with words and pantomime. The cost of fixing the bicycle, it seemed, would be six hundred escudos (about twenty-four dollars). Without the bicycle Marco could not get work. It was impossible for her to save the money to pay for the bicycle. Ahead, then, lay nothing but ruin, but that was the lot of people like her in the world and she could do nothing but continue to struggle and trust in the infinite mercy of the good God.

I was quite touched at this and might have given her a check for the repair of the bicycle had I not happened to catch a glimpse of Marco's face.

He was looking at his wife in pure admiration, as if she had, by this display, far exceeded even the talents for acting which he already knew she possessed.

So I withheld the offer of money and murmured a few words of sympathy. Maria blushed with vexation and scurried off into the living room (the conversation having taken place in the kitchen), to return announcing triumphantly that Tully had thrown up on the carpet.

Plainly, in her mind, no dog with a master of generous habits would do such a thing. Furthermore, she explained that the carpet belonged to the senhor from whom we were renting the house and was an expensive carpet. The tablecloth off which we had dined was also his, and he had given her to understand that whoever might rent the house must provide themselves with linen, for his linens were not to be used by the tenants.

I found a bucket and some cloths and went to the living room to clean up the mess. Maria was immediately repentant. She had been vexed because I had not offered the money for the bicycle, but she did not want a demonstration of my

American self-sufficiency. She turned sharply to her husband and rattled an order at him in Portuguese. He took away the bucket and the cloths over my protest and cleaned up the carpet.

Then Hazel took a hand in the game. She examined the tablecloth, announced that she did not like it and would buy several more suitable to her taste on the morrow. She called Maria and, after I had opened a trunk or two, gave her some sheets and asked her to make up the beds for the children. They were beautiful sheets of good quality linen, green ones and pink ones—rich, aristocratic American sheets (if adjective and noun can be taken as agreeing with each other).

Maria was greatly impressed. She handed the sheets reverently to Celita and told her to make the beds—a nice piece of finesse serving notice that bedmaking was not in her sphere though she would supervise such operations.

Finally we got the children in their pajamas—Kevin, Patricia, Christopher, and Arabella. They knelt down before the fireplace to say their prayers, kissed us, and stood hesitating before Maria.

But Christopher is not a boy to withhold his heart.

He rushed to Maria, threw his arms somewhere around her knees, and with his face sparkling with love said, "Good night, Maria." She stooped to pick him up in her strong brown arms and all her defenses were down.

"Good night, little one," she said in Portuguese, and he laid his head happily on her shoulder.

Maria turned to the others. Tricia was squirming with excitement at finding a new friend. Kevin was protecting Arabella, who had got behind him and was about to swoon with nervousness. Maria picked up Arabella, who will never go to anyone until she's known them for weeks, and Arabella was so surprised that she didn't let out a peep.

"*Boa noite, senhor y senhora, ate amanha,*" she said to us, and led the children off to bed.

We were accepted, at least for the time being, though there might be problems ahead.

7.

WE HAD BEEN BUT TWO DAYS
in our Portuguese home when I had a heart attack. I say a heart
attack, but it may have been a bout of malaria or a whiff of
carbon monoxide or a return of that strep throat which in the
United States had crept so astonishingly into my arms and
lungs.

It was late at night, and since the weather was still foul, I
was stoking up the little furnace which heated the house and
particularly the bedroom wing. I wanted it to remain alight
all night, for I abominate cold bedrooms. Suddenly, standing
crouched with a shovel full of coke in my hands, I became as
weak as a kitten. Perspiration broke out on my forehead. I
trembled and tried to say something but could not. My throat
seemed to have swollen up and my jaws pained. I dropped the
shovel and groped my way to the living room where Hazel
was tidying up preparatory to retiring.

"Something's the matter with me," I said. "I must lie down."

I wobbled off toward the bedroom and recalled that car-
bon-monoxide gas is given off in dangerous quantities by coke-
burning furnaces, if the ventilation is poor.

"The children," I croaked. "The furnace is leaking carbon
monoxide. Open the doors of their rooms and the windows."
I was so weak that I could do nothing myself to assist her.
Hazel tried Kevin's bedroom door. But the doorknob turned
in her hand without operating the lock. She pounded on the

door. But Kevin once asleep is not to be awakened by less than the end of the earth, and that a noisy end. Hazel shouted, and I dragged myself out of my deathbed to add a feeble cry or two and twiddled with the door handle. The uproar woke Maria and her husband, Marco. He, stout and handsome young fellow, kept to his room, but Maria got up.

"*Que pas?*" she demanded in much excitement.

"Carbon monoxide," I croaked. "Todos blooming well dying."

Whether this conveyed any sense or not I do not know. Maria swore furiously at the door handle and went away and returned with a large screw driver. She pulled the doorknob and its shaft out of the door and inserted the screw driver—she was seemingly an old hand at this trick—and fooled with the lock. Hazel, meanwhile, had gone outside, in a night wild enough to quail a pirate, to the front of the house, and managed to open the bedroom window. She hoisted herself up on the sill and fell with a horrifying noise into the pitch-black room. In the same moment Maria managed to open the door and turn on the light.

Kevin was happily asleep, his legs pillowed on the back of Christopher, who was also asleep though not so happy. By now I was near collapse once more, so I staggered off to bed and lay down to die. Hazel checked Patricia and Arabella and found them still breathing and healthy.

Maria returned to bed, swearing prettily in Portuguese, and Hazel came in to see me.

I was lying on my back across the bed, bathed in perspiration. My jaws ached as they do when one, unused to a rigorous climate, is exposed to zero cold. I seemed to be able to get but an inch of breath when I needed several feet. I believed I was dying, and I was furious about it.

Perhaps when I really die I shall be afraid of that tremendous leap in the dark which we all of us must take. But on the two occasions when I thought I was dying I was merely angry —the first time because my wife was out buying a hat; the second time because it seemed to me the purest knavery that I should be struck down, snatched into eternity, leaving my wife and children in a foreign land where they had not a friend and could not speak a word of the language.

"How are you feeling?" Hazel asked.

"Get Bill if I check out," I said, and closed my eyes. Bill is an old newspaper friend in Los Angeles and could be relied upon to get Hazel and the children back from Portugal if necessary.

"I'm going to call a doctor," said Hazel, and went off to rouse Maria once again. But by the time this had been achieved I was feeling better. The terrible ache in my neck which extended down the chest and arm muscles went. I began to breathe again without effort, and the weakness and perspiring passed. And suddenly I had an overwhelming appetite for candy.

When Hazel reappeared with Maria it was to find me sitting on the bed and demanding whether there was any chocolate in the house. Hazel found two half-pound bars and I began to stuff big chunks in my mouth, chewing on them and swallowing them in lumps, such was the voracity of my appetite.

Maria went off calling on God to witness that the English senhor was mad. For what other reason would he arise in the middle of the night, bat down the door of the children's bedroom, and then return to bed and start eating chocolates?

Hazel settled down, having first made me promise that I would wake her up if I was going to die. I said I'd try, if given decent notice of my exit.

The next morning we sent for a doctor.

I have always had difficulty in describing symptoms to doctors even in English. In French the difficulties were almost insurmountable. The doctor who came was cheerful and bright but could speak no English though he professed to know a little French. I told him I was sick, which was obvious, but when he asked me where I was sick I could not explain. The French words for chest, arms, throat, legs fled from me if indeed I had ever known them. I could not even remember the French word for pain. All my French lessons had dealt with aunts and uncles, pens, gardens, ink and inkwells, and the windows and doors which one constantly demanded should be opened or shut *s'il vous plâit*. Nobody had ever had a heart attack in French to my knowledge.

"Je pense que j'ai le mal coeur," I said. *"Le soir dernier . . ."* and here I ran out. *"Le soir dernier,"* I blundered on, *"je suis mort."*

"Vous avez fait la résurrection magnifique," replied the doctor. We stumbled around, butchering French, throwing in a little pidgin English and Portuguese, and getting more and more desperate and more and more lost. Finally the doctor got me to understand that I should open my mouth while he looked at my throat.

I knew what was coming then.

It was just like being back in the States.

He spotted my strep throat which had returned and gave me a prescription to deal with this. Then he looked at all the children who all had colds and prescribed for them. Everybody in Portugal, he assured us, had a cold. The Portuguese get a cold in October and it seems to last them through until the middle of April when it disappears with the mid spring to be replaced by hay fever.

When the doctor departed I still did not know what kind of an attack I had suffered the previous night, though he asked me to call him, irrespective of the hour, if it recurred.

I found myself calling on him pretty often. Every visitor to Portugal suffers, because of the severe diet change, from massive indigestion. And so I called on him about this. He prescribed a brand of stomach powder, which I later found sells by the ton to new arrivals. You may spot a new arrival in Portugal in any restaurant by the bottle of stomach powder which he places on the table as soon as he sits down. Again I had to call upon the doctor when Tully bit me.

Tully, from the beginning, took a firm dislike to Portugal. His whole personality altered so that he changed from a quiet and amiable animal with a fondness for Bach and Beethoven (he would, in the States, crouch beside my set whenever I was playing the works of these composers) into a surly brute, uncertain of temper and difficult to handle. One morning, finding he had slept that night on the couch in the living room, although he knew all furniture forbidden him, I clouted him for the misdeed. He snapped back at me, quick as a snake, and inflicted a three-inch gash perhaps a quarter of an inch deep in the palm of my hand.

The doctor bandaged it and I went subsequently to his office many times for dressing. His office was in a building called The House of the Two Fishermen, in Cascais. Most of his patients were fishermen who had hooked themselves, or cut themselves with knives, or got fish bones embedded in their flesh. As my French and Portuguese improved I was able to converse more freely with him.

"The fishermen keep you pretty busy?" I asked one day.

"Only when the fishing is bad," he replied. "When it is good, my office is empty. I have had a man run out of here while I was dressing a wound in his arm because the cry had gone up that there was a big shoal of fish four miles offshore. He returned two days later. The wound was then septic but he was very happy. He had caught a ton and a half of fish, but he was in danger of losing his arm as a result."

Since Hazel's baby was due in a couple of months after our arrival in Portugal, I had to find a doctor immediately who would take care of her and deliver the child.

We consulted several people, most of whom advised getting a doctor in Lisbon, hinting that local doctors were not much better than midwives. But a doctor in Lisbon would not be much use to us. We were a dozen miles or more from Lisbon and had no car.

When the baby came, it would be a difficult matter to get into Lisbon to the hospital for delivery, for I did not know how reliable the taxi services were. Eventually we discovered a doctor who practiced in Lisbon but had a maternity clinic in Monte Estoril about four miles from Malveira da Serra. I went along to interview him and once again came up against the formidable language barrier.

He was a big and heavy-set man, in his late fifties or early sixties. His maternity clinic was in an old converted villa. The gardens around it, though large, were woefully lacking in care, and the building itself needed painting. Some of the shutters looked as though they were about to fall off the second- and third-story windows. I had my doubts that this was the place for Hazel before I even saw the doctor. They increased rather than abated as our interview progressed.

"*O senhor fala Inglis?*" I asked, and he shook his massive head.

"*Français?*"

Again no.

If there was one thing of which I was incapable it was telling anyone in Portuguese that my wife was in her seventh month of pregnancy. Yet somehow or other I had to convey this important fact to the doctor.

I got out of my chair and said, "wife," and reinforced this by adding the word "*ma femme.*" He nodded. I made a huge parabola in the air before my stomach and shuffled up and down his office in what I hoped was a good imitation of the flat-footed, cautious gait of a pregnant woman. I fancy I caught a twinkle in the doctor's eyes. Then, suddenly inspired, I gave him a transcript of the medical report on Hazel from her doctor in California. He looked this over with growing interest and excitement. He summoned his nurse and showed it to her, and they exclaimed together in admiration over the details.

"*Sabada,*" he said. "*Onze horas,*" by which I took him to mean that Hazel was to come and see him on Saturday at eleven o'clock.

We were there by taxi at ten thirty. The waiting room was full of Portuguese women in various stages of pregnancy. They fell quiet and all looked at Hazel, judging her size, and speculating on The Date.

She, in turn, looked them over, too, and I was conscious that there was established, in that moment, between my American wife and these Portuguese women, that secret, strong liaison, sympathy and understanding, which grows immediately between pregnant women whatever their nationality or situation in life. Then all turned and looked at me. Bearded and balding, I was the lone man in a room of perhaps fifteen very pregnant ladies. The look they gave me was one of accusation and reproof mixed with saintly acceptance of enormous injury. I lost my nerve and went outside and smoked a cigarette with the taxi driver.

"You are not feeling well, senhor?" the taxi driver asked. He spoke a fair amount of English which could be understood if you realized that he accented the words and pitched them in what I can only describe as a Portuguese meter and tune.

"I feel all right," I replied.

"This pregnancy," he said, "it is hard on men. It causes a sadness of the soul and a heaviness of the stomach. You should drink a little red wine to sustain yourself."

"It's hard on women, too," I replied.

He flicked a cigarette butt into a jungle of geraniums.

"It is worse for men," he said. "Women are used to it. After all, it is what they are for. But men. . . . It takes a nerve of iron. I know many men who take to their beds when their wives are being delivered. It is dangerous for a man to be about at such a time."

I was delighted with this information. The belief that men should go to bed during the delivery of children is one of the oldest in human history and is to be found in the folklore of almost every nation, though I have never found any support for it among modern doctors. Still, they do not know everything.

"The doctor is good?" I asked.

"Very good," said the taxi driver, whose name was Toni. "He delivered all my children—I have four. No trouble. If you have no money he says 'forget about it.' He takes care of women who are not married. He keeps them in the maternity wards for a week at least to feed them up. Sometimes they want to go home to look after the other children. But he demands that they stay and get their strength back. And he does not charge them if they are poor. Everybody loves him. If his car is broken down we drive him for nothing. The people bring him fish and flour when they can. He is the father of these people here."

When Hazel came out she was radiant.

"What a wonderful doctor," she said. "What do you mean he doesn't speak English? He speaks English as well as you or I."

I puzzled about that a great deal and came to the conclusion that the doctor had just wanted to see what a husband would do, deprived of language, to indicate that his wife was pregnant.

What especially pleased Hazel was that the doctor did not scold her because of her weight or demand that she stay on a rigorous diet to keep her weight down.

"I can eat anything I want," she said.

The doctor's fee for the examination was eighty cents.

We went to a restaurant in Estoril and Hazel ate three cream puffs, for, when pregnant, she has a huge appetite for sweetmeats and fruit.

I had a spartan cup of tea.

The Resurrection of Rover

8.

So WITHIN TWO WEEKS OF AR-
rival in Portugal we had found a home, a doctor for Hazel,
had a domestic staff to take care of us, had so far obtained the
upper hand of this staff, but there still remained one big problem to be dealt with. That was the problem of our car, Rover,
which lay smashed on the dock in faraway New York.

As the days went by, the problem of Rover grew more
acute. We came to realize that nice as our home was, it was
also isolated. We were some four miles from the nearest place
with shops—Estoril. To be sure we had about us a lovely
forest of pines through which we could wander at will. We
had an unrivaled view of the mouth of the Tagus and its junc-
tion with the Atlantic. We had ample gardens in which to
stroll and meditate. But we were like a little colony in space,
cut off from restaurants and bookstores and post offices and
doctors and curio shops and other activities and delights because of the lack of a car. Such isolation becomes, after a while,
mildly depressing.

Toni, the taxi driver, would take us down to Estoril and
back for five dollars. But one cannot spend five dollars a day
on taxi fares and survive in the literary business. Once Maria
and her husband went to Cascais, a village perhaps a half mile
nearer to us than Estoril, in a taxi and returned. I was puzzled
that out of wages of twenty dollars a month they could afford
such luxury, but soon learned that in Portugal there are two

kinds of taxi prices—those for the Portuguese and those for the foreigners.

Maria's taxi fare was a dollar-fifty whereas mine was always five dollars. I tackled Toni about this and he agreed that in future I would pay only three dollars. To pay what my servant paid would be beneath my dignity. Three dollars would preserve my status in life and Toni made no apology whatsoever for previously charging five. This was some progress in obtaining transportation at a reasonable cost. But it was not enough. I wanted to explore Portugal and I wasn't going to do it by taxi. I must have a car.

Accordingly I got in touch with the agents of the steamship company and asked them to have my wrecked Rover shipped from New York to Lisbon, since I had already paid the fare. They agreed smoothly. I had previously discovered there was a garage in Lisbon staffed with good mechanics who were capable of fixing anything that was fixable.

With the passage of time, I began to assure myself that Rover, though dropped from a sling some forty feet to a dock, might yet be fixable. So we sent for the car and in the interim wrote to the shipping company saying that we held them responsible for the damage. They wrote back referring to the "alleged" damage and saying that their responsibility was limited to a hundred dollars.

I wrote demanding to know whether they would be satisfied with the offer of just enough to buy a rowboat in return for the wrecking of one of their luxury liners. This letter, though perfectly sensible and to the point, brought no reply.

Finally we learned that Rover was being shipped on an Italian tramp steamer but not to expect the arrival too soon. It was as well that we didn't, for the tramp steamer took eight weeks to cross the Atlantic. I went down to the shipping agents to get the bill of lading when the ship arrived. When I saw it my heart sank. It contained the following statement: "This car is a complete wreck and the company accepts no responsibility for it whatever."

I began to have misgivings. It might have been wiser to write off Rover as a dead loss, attempt to recover compensation through the law courts if necessary, and in the meantime obtain the return of the two hundred and fifty dollars which I paid for the shipping of the car. I signed the necessary papers to obtain possession of the car and went down to the garage with whom I had previously discussed the whole matter.

Senhor Garcia, a director of the garage, agreed to come down to the dock with me to help get Rover unloaded and towed to the garage.

It is not often that a director of such an establishment goes out to attend to a wrecked car, and I was very gratified at his concern. But then it is not often that a car is wrecked by being dropped from a ship onto a dock, and I suppose there was some curiosity as well as courtesy behind his gesture.

We arrived at the dock and located the Italian tramp and went aboard. On the port side, forward, there was a heavy tarpaulin, glistening with salt. Senhor Garcia summoned the first mate who summoned the captain, who piped all hands through the bosun, and we stood around this tarpaulin as men stand around the sarcophagus of some hero returning to his homeland for burial.

The first mate signaled to the bosun, who nodded to the seamen, who began to take the funeral wrappings off Rover. It was plain that Rover had been a source of speculation among the crew all the way across the Atlantic. What kind of man, they asked themselves, would ship a completely wrecked car from New York to Lisbon? What was the secret of this car?

Was there, perhaps embedded somewhere in the body work, some precious thing—a fabulous hidden diamond being smuggled from one country to another, or a priceless canvas, or perhaps a ton and a half of heroin?

The tarpaulin was removed and everyone turned to look at me.

I nearly wept.

Rover was the most bruised and broken and battered thing I have ever seen. The wheels were ovals and the body was crumpled as brown paper becomes crumpled when roughly handled. I loved that car. It was an old friend, a comrade of mine and of my family. It was a living thing for all of us, and I had left it heavily wounded and dying, on the New York dock, and then on a long voyage across the Atlantic. I walked over to Rover and touched one of the bent and rusted and torn fenders. The crew stood around in silence. One or two removed their hats.

The mate cleared his throat. "There is a good price to be had for wrecked automobiles in Lisbon, senhor?" he asked.

"No," I snapped.

"I do not understand," said the mate. He pointed to the car, looked at the crew, and shrugged.

"It is our car," I said. "We love it."

Such a statement among a colder-blooded people would have marked me as eccentric to the point of madness. But the Italians immediately understood. The mate turned to the silent crew and said "*Amor*" and they looked now tenderly at the car and at me with faces of compassion.

"I understand, senhor," said the mate. "At home I have a little Isetta. It is like a jeweled bird. When I am not on the ocean I take my Isetta through the countryside to see the flowers and the mountains and the trees. We talk to each other and enjoy these things, my little jeweled bird and I."

We did not embrace physically, but the immediate understanding between us was as if we had.

The captain now wished to express his sympathy in some way. He knew that the sight of my mangled car was hard on me and invited me down to his cabin for a drink of wine. But I did not want to leave the deck until the car had been put ashore, and so refused his offer. The men removed the tarpaulin as one would remove a bandage. They put slings around the car, not roughly, scraping the wire rope along the metal, but gently and with a desire not to hurt.

The captain himself addressed the hoist operator, begging him that no more hurt be done to so heavily stricken a thing. The car was raised gently from the deck, swung gently through the air, and put down—on top of the customs office.

"Why have they put Rover on the roof of that building?" I asked Senhor Garcia.

"It is necessary to get a clearance through the customs first," he replied. "You have a triptych or a *carnet de passage?*"

"No," I said. "The Portuguese consul assured me that these documents were not necessary in Portugal. A permit can be issued here for a few dollars to permit the car to be landed."

"We shall see," said Senhor Garcia.

Like a diplomat with a delicate point to win, he interviewed the customs officials. They came out and looked at the car on the roof and looked at me with suspicion. They went back into their offices. More consultations took place. For an hour I was in an agony of uncertainty, wondering whether I had shipped Rover from New York merely to have it become a kind of monument for all time—or until the sea winds rusted it to nothing—on top of the customs building in Lisbon. Eventually Senhor Garcia returned with a slip of paper which constituted a permit to keep the car in Portugal for two months. The permit, he said, could be renewed for a further period.

Now came the appalling task of getting Rover from the Lisbon dock to the garage where the mechanics could repair it. A winch truck was summoned, the car lowered from the roof, and the front end hoisted up in the air. All this was done in the presence of a crowd of perhaps eighty or a hundred spectators, fascinated by the madness of the bearded man who had brought this junk heap all the way from New York at enormous expense.

The winch truck moved forward and there was a scream of agony from Rover as if its bones were being split in some medieval torture instrument. The scream was produced by the rear wheels being dragged without turning across the surface of the dock. I implored the winch truck driver to stop and get out.

"The wheels are locked in gear," I said. "I'll put her into neutral."

But first came the problem of getting into Rover to achieve this. The front doors were pleated so I could not get in. Only one rear door could be wrenched open. I climbed into the back seat and slid into the front part of the car. The dashboard had been driven back by the impact of the fall a foot or more, so there was scarcely room to squeeze behind the steering wheel, which was woefully bent. I felt around for the clutch pedal, depressed it, and struggled with the gearshift.

Nothing happened.

The car was locked in gear. There was nothing to do but ride in Rover with one foot on the clutch so as to disengage the gears until the garage was reached.

In my youth I did a great deal of single-handed sailing, particularly in the Caribbean. I have been out in some wild seas, with a chop from the southwest fighting it out with a heavy easterly swell from the Atlantic. I was never seasick. But I got seasick riding Rover from the dock to the garage.

One trouble was that the front end kept swinging around (yawing is the sailor's term) from port to starboard on the winch. Added to this was the fact that the egg-shaped rear wheels got out of synchronization with each other. When they were in mesh with each other, the effect was of riding up and down on the riffles of a gigantic washboard. But when they got at cross-purposes with each other, I not only rode up and down but was thrown simultaneously from port to starboard in a heavy roll. Destroyer sailormen have told me since that it was exactly the same as being in the crow's-nest of a tin can dashing through an Atlantic swell on a wild February night. So I became seasick. But I was enough of a sailor (or wrecked-car navigator) to keep my foot on the clutch though a sweat of agony from nausea poured off my face and the whole of Lisbon, statues and tiled house fronts and ornate balconies, revolved around me.

When we got to the garage I went away for a necessary five minutes and returned pale and shaking. The mechanics of the garage had gathered around the car. They had been repairing cars for many years, most of them, but had never seen one in such a condition. Senhor Garcia explained that it had been dropped on a dock and their professional curiosity was aroused. What, they wondered, happened to a car weighing a ton and a half after a fall of forty or more feet onto a concrete dock? They put Rover on a jack and hoisted it up in the air and swarmed underneath, exclaiming over the various injuries which had been inflicted on it.

Senhor Garcia came over to me. "You had better go home,"

he said, like the surgeon in a hospital. "We will know more tomorrow."

I went home to a very sleepless night.

I was early at the garage the following day, and Senhor Garcia took me without a word into his office, seated me, and gave me a cigarette.

"It is hopeless," he said quietly. "The frame is bent. The transmission is wrecked and so is the differential. The engine block is cracked. The radiator is useless. The steering box..." He shrugged. "It is useless," he concluded. "Forget about repairs. They are impossible."

He saw the stricken look on my face, and, grieved that he had to be the bearer of such dismal news, searched around in his mind for some crumb of comfort.

"There is only one thing which was undamaged," he said. "A memento. I have kept it aside for you."

I brightened a little at this, and he went to a cupboard and brought out Arabella's potty chair.

I looked at it in surprise and the thought occurred to me that were the world to be destroyed in some holocaust, the only artifact to survive and be found by visitors from another planet might well be Arabella's potty chair. I had never suspected such fortitude in so humble an article.

"Arabella will not be pleased," I murmured, for Arabella did not like her chair. We returned to the car.

"It is quite impossible to save it?" I asked.

"Impossible," said Senhor Garcia.

"Then I must leave it here," I said.

"That is also impossible," said Senhor Garcia.

"What do you mean?" I cried.

"You have brought the car in. You must take it out. That is the law," he said.

"Good heavens!" I said. "Surely I am not condemned to carry a wrecked automobile around Europe, from country to country, at enormous expense, looking for a place to bury it?"

"That is unfortunately the law," said Senhor Garcia. "The car may remain here for two months under the temporary permit. Then it must be removed."

"How about Spain?" I asked.

"The same."

"France, England, Ireland?"

"The same."

"Could I just push it off a cliff somewhere?"

"No," said Senhor Garcia. "You could perhaps hire a barge and take it out to sea and dump it in the ocean. But there is the difficulty of a permit to ensure that you do not dump it in a part where it would constitute a hazard to shipping."

"Maybe I could dump it in the path of one of the liners of the shipping company who wrecked it in the first instance," I said. "It might wreck one of their ships. That would be poetic justice."

"Not without a permit," said Senhor Garcia.

"This is fantastic," I expostulated. "You do not—you cannot —mean what you are saying."

"Alas," said Senhor Garcia, "these are the facts. If you refuse to remove the car after the two months of the permit has expired, it will be impounded by the customs, you will have to pay storage on it, and you, on leaving the country, will have to pay the tax on a new car. Otherwise you will not be allowed to leave Portugal."

It all sounded so asinine as to be perfectly true, for the peak of asininity, in my experience, is an essential of any government service.

"Then," I said firmly, "the car must be fixed."

"Impossible," said Senhor Garcia.

"Senhor," I said, "the might and splendor of Portugal in its great days were not achieved by men who kept saying 'impossible' every hour on the hour. The great Da Gama did not say 'impossible' when he slipped out of that river there on a foul night to sail to the Indies. Henry, the Navigator, Prince of Portugal and of all seamen, did not say 'impossible' when he speculated on the existence of a land across the western ocean. The great captains of your caravels, threading their way across unknown and ominous seas to the riches of China, did not say 'impossible' in the sweltering heat of the Indian Ocean when God's wind had died and the pitch bubbled in the seams of the deck." I went on in this vein at some length and my effort took effect.

A look of inspiration and determination came into the face of Senhor Garcia. He rose and brought his fist down on the seat of Arabella's potty chair, which withstood the blow without wincing.

"All right," he said, "we can do it. We mechanics of Portugal can do it. No one else could."

We shook hands, and I left him to the task.

9.

THE GARAGEMEN, CALLING UPON the ancient daring and courage and enterprise of the Portuguese race, finally restored Rover. They had to install a new engine and pretty well rebuild the chassis, and there were times, looking at the skeleton of the car, stripped down to its bent frame, when thinking it would never be put together again, that I denounced myself as an idiot to employ my dwindling money in such an enterprise. But finally they got it all together and were amazed by their own achievement. Rover sparkled under new paint. Even the leather seat covering had been renewed. How glad I felt that I had not deserted this old comrade. And how shocked I felt when I got the bill.

It amounted to one thousand dollars. And eighteen hundred was all I had between me and the arrival of my next royalty check, which was some months off.

I paid for Rover and drove out to the house, at times exultant and at times plunged into an abyss of depression. The children were on tiptoe with excitement, awaiting the arrival of the car. They rushed screaming out of the house as wild as Indians when I came up the drive, and one and all demanded to be taken for a ride.

They climbed in, saying, "Good old Rover," and caressing the upholstery. Christopher was so excited he kept rolling his head from side to side on the back of the seat and saying, "Rover's well. Rover's well. Hurray! Hurray! Rover's well."

Finally we all took up this chant to the astonishment of Maria and Marco and Celita and Tomaso.

But Maria was just as pleased as we. The Senhor had an automobile. He was a man of something more than whisky distinction. Certainly the various merchants from which she bought food would hear about this beautiful car in a quite casual manner when she next did her shopping.

I took the children for their ride. When we got back I told Hazel how much the car had cost and that at that moment we had only eight hundred dollars in the bank and the rent was due. Furthermore, I would have to find six hundred dollars to get a *carnet de passage* issued for the car so it could remain in Portugal longer than allowed by the temporary permit.

"What that means," said Hazel, "is that we really have no money at all."

"Right," I replied.

We thought about this awhile. Maybe some film producer would decide to produce one of my books and cable me an offer of perhaps a hundred thousand dollars.

This happens constantly to other authors, and it was about my turn. Or maybe the *Reader's Digest* or some magazine would take one of my books in condensed form and send me a check for a few thousand dollars. This also has happened to authors within living memory. Indeed it had once happened to me. So it could happen again, and I pointed out the possibilities to Hazel as we went somewhat optimistically to bed.

Authors, wherever they may be, wait constantly and anxiously on the mails. Around royalty time—which occurs every six months—any man you see standing in the road in your neighborhood pretending to be bird watching is an author waiting for the arrival of the mailman.

Writers live on mail. Apart from letters telling them whether a piece they have written has been accepted or rejected, they wait in piteous anxiety for reviews of their work. They read these reviews through and if they are good, they read the book through themselves to see how the reviewer found them so wise and witty when they weren't conscious of being wise and witty at all. If the review is bad, they suffer from stomach cramps and trembling of the limbs and some go to bed for a week. I, myself, faced with bad reviews, have made it my Christian duty to say a prayer for the repose of the soul of the reviewer.

In the week that followed the resurrection of Rover we waited with special anxiety for the mail. Our mailman in Portugal, having to come four miles from the post office in Cascais, had bought himself a little motor bicycle. That is to say it was a bicycle from the vintage year of 1912 equipped with a small single-stroke motor which popped with every four revolutions of the crank, driving him forward at a pleasant eight miles an hour. We used to sit in the living room after breakfast, with the huge French windows open if the day was fair, waiting for the most exciting noise of the day—the uncertain pop pop pop of the mailman's motor bicycle.

When we first got our house the mailman used to arrive at about eleven in the morning. But there were many false alarms, for it seemed that other miscreants in the neighborhood had the same kind of motor bicycles. I would hear the exciting pop pop pop and say to Hazel, "The mail's come. Throw the children out so I can read it in comfort." And then the mail would not arrive. The pop pop pop we had heard was the milkman's motor bicycle, or the electricity man, or some other person. But gradually our ears got attuned and we could recognize the noise made by the mailman's machine as readily as a violinist can distinguish B sharp from C natural.

It is a well-known phenomenon of the writing business that when the writer most needs mail—when he is broke and well behind with payments on the necessities of life—he either gets none, or the mailman, discovering his predicament, delivers his mail exceedingly late in the day.

This fate now awaited us. The day after Rover's return no mail arrived by eleven, by twelve, by one, or even two o'clock. I summoned Maria and Celita and Tomaso and Marco to consult them about what could have happened to the mailman.

They seemed unconcerned, not realizing that their own fate was to some extent involved in what he had in the mailbag for me. I discovered the route he took from Cascais to Malveira and set out in Rover to find him, for I was sure the wretch had dropped in at some little tavern upon the road and was now wassailing and possibly losing all his letters, having grown careless of his responsibilities.

I found him sitting on the moorlands about two miles away. He was bandaging the rear wheel of his motor bicycle. He had a length of extremely dirty rag, no doubt full of germs, which he was tying around the tire on the rear wheel. I knew, without any conversation, that he had had a puncture, but I had never seen anybody bandage a puncture before.

I exchanged condolences with him, encouraged him in his attempts, and inquired if he had any letter for me. He did. It was from my agent in the kind of envelope in which agents usually send money—they use square envelopes for money letters and long envelopes for letters saying that they'd read my last book but . . .

I flung all my poise to the winds and opened the letter. Inside was a note from the telephone company in southern California saying they had been over their books, I owed them fifty-one cents, and would I be kind enough to remit the amount. I felt as though I had been hit in the stomach with a battering ram, and staggering off blindly to Rover, I drove away leaving the mailman still bandaging his bicycle on the road.

This kind of thing went on for a week. The mail was shockingly late every day, for the bandage on the rear wheel of the motor bicycle did not stand up well and the mailman was not wealthy enough to afford a new outer casing. When the mail did arrive, it usually contained only a request for the renewal of a subscription to a magazine which on the moment I hated heartily—the editor and all his works and pomps. Or there was a circular from the Cunard Steam-Ship Company announcing a new sailing. (I got on their circular list as sea serpent editor of the *Rocky Mountain Herald* and had asked them to have the captains of the *Queen Mary* and so on keep a sharp lookout for sea serpents.) Or it might contain a request from a librarian to speak to a group meeting in southern California a month before the date of the arrival of the letter. Nothing much to any of this, and gradually I faced up to the inevitable.

"This can't go on," I told Hazel. "I don't know for sure, but they probably still have debtors' prison in places like Portugal. I'll have to sit down and write another book."

And that was it. Somerset Maugham and Steinbeck and Hemingway and others might be able to live at ease in foreign parts, playing a little *chemin de fer* or maybe killing swordfish, but I was Wibberley, and wherever I went I had to pull out my old typewriter and write another book for groceries, and leave *chemin de fer* and cocktails on a marble terrace overlooking the Tagus severely alone.

"What are you going to write a book about?" Kevin asked, for he takes a great interest in my subject matter.

"If I knew anything about it," I said, "I'd write a cookbook. A fellow can live for years off a cookbook. You kids ought to watch Maria and find out how she cooks things, and then I could write it all up and you could go to college.

"But since I don't know anything about cooking I'll write about something I do know—the American Revolutionary War." I immediately began warming to the subject. I could hear the groaning of an inn sign in the city of Boston in the year 1774 and see the snow flashing in the street outside the lighted window of a tavern. Out of the gloom a figure staggered down the street toward the window wrapped in a coachman's cloak. He had a thin mouth and prominent yellow teeth and it was plain that even death could not make him beautiful. Portugal and Maria and Hazel and the children all disappeared, and I looked at this man and wondered what his name was and what he was doing there.

"The Senhor is sick?" asked Maria in a whisper.

"No," said Hazel, "the Senhor is writing a book," and she hustled everybody out of the room and I started to write the book.

It took me several weeks, and in all that time I lived spiritually in Boston and the Caribbean and the North Carolina mountains which were the locale of my story, and had only remote and quite unreal contacts with Portugal. The news that I was writing a book soon spread to all my neighbors. A Portuguese lady living nearby offered me the use of her house in which to write, and the mailman began inquiring how I was coming along, and every morning Maria would look at the size of the pile of pages written.

Even Tomaso, when he learned that I could not stop in the middle of the Battle of Bunker Hill, with the Grenadiers sweeping forward, drums rolling, and bayonets bright in the sunlight, to acknowledge his bows found a way of sneaking past me, though I discovered that when he had got out of my line of view he would bow and take off his beret anyway.

When the book was done, I sent it off and we started waiting on the mail again. By now we had only fifty dollars in the bank, and it was essential to watch this very carefully. The situation was not really desperate. There were good friends in America who would come through with a loan. But one likes to earn rather than borrow, and so we were anxious.

It was necessary, then, to look into the household accounts and see where any economies could be effected.

When we first came to the house Maria had required thirty dollars a week for groceries. Then this had risen to thirty-five, to forty, and finally to forty-five. I waited for a leveling off but always more grocery money was needed. And it seemed that in addition to the money I gave her other money was needed for eggs and milk and bread which were paid for separately. Then one terrible day I made the discovery, long hidden carefully by Maria, that she had been charging certain items at a rather fancy grocery store in Cascais which handled things like corn flakes and bacon, unobtainable in the public market.

Maria went to the market for us three times a week. Whenever she returned, she proudly showed us some little trifle which she had bought for herself. Presumably it was bought out of the grocery money and we shrugged off these little purchases as being the custom of the country.

There was a pair of thin gold earrings one week, and the next week, a gold ring with a cheap kind of stone in it. Following that there was a quite handsome enameled pin. We only began worrying when one week Marco, her young and handsome husband, turned up with a gleaming, beautiful new bicycle which would have cost Maria a year's salary to buy. This was followed by Maria buying Marco a beautiful jacket with a collar of fur, the kind of jacket I would have loved for myself but could not possibly afford. Another week Maria returned from her shopping with several yards of handsome English worsted which she told Hazel would be used to make a new dress for herself. Hazel looked at the worsted sadly. She had never been able to buy such material, but Maria assured her that in Portugal it was to be had quite reasonably.

Then came the final blow. The beds in the house were somewhat worn and the mattresses sagged in the middle. Hazel has a weak back and it finally gave out on her. The muscles developed a massive cramp because of the peculiarities of the mattress. That was the week when Hazel, staggering in a crippled state around the house, answered the door to find that a new innerspring mattress was being delivered to the house.

"Darling," she said to me, deeply touched, "you shouldn't have done it."

"I didn't do it," I replied.

And I hadn't. It was Maria's mattress. Marco, it seemed, was uncomfortable on their mattress, and she had been saving up to buy a new one. It was part of her constant campaign to keep the affections of her young and handsome husband.

We now began to entertain the darkest of suspicions concerning Maria. We concluded that half our grocery money was being spent on baubles with which to decorate or dress herself or on gifts for Marco, all with the object of keeping him, a faithful but too handsome and young a spouse, by her side.

But what could we do? I hate to judge people on suspicion or circumstances which are suspicious.

I would not shrink from the matter if I had any proof of this gross misappropriation of our household funds. But how could I obtain proof—hard, uncontrovertible proof?

I did what I could. I told Maria that she was in no circumstances to charge any food at the fancy grocery and that in future I would give her only forty dollars a week, out of which she must supply all the groceries and pay for the bread and eggs. I would pay for the milk out of my own pocket.

She received this news all a-smoulder, and at the end of the week, when the eggs had to be paid for, kept saying aloud like a child that she had no money with which to pay for them. I paid no attention. She had had forty dollars with which to pay for the eggs and if she had seen fit to make a payment on Marco's bicycle instead, that was her affair. She would not get a cent of egg money out of me.

Maria was a clever woman and one of some resource. She took each of the children aside in the kitchen, fixed them a bowl of soup, told them she had no money for the eggs, and broke into tears.

Kevin is a generous boy and if he does not become president of the United States, it will be because out of pity for his opponent he threw a block of votes to him at a crucial point in the campaign. He went away to his money box and gave Maria the contents.

Next it was Tricia's turn. But Tricia, though but six, is still a woman and knows the wiles of women. She drank the garlic soup, looked calmly at Maria's tears, and said she was saving her money for a six-gun. She was ejected in some haste from the kitchen.

It was Christopher's turn next. He also received, as Maria well knew, a small sum each week for doing various chores around the household—one of these, incidentally, being to report when Arabella had wet her pants.

But Christopher had not yet reached the sad age when he could reckon money. To Christopher money is money and fifty centavos (if the coin is bright) is as goodly a sum as a million dollars. A pity it is that the world and I must teach him differently and so make him miserable.

Having heard from Maria that she must have three dollars for eggs and his father, the Senhor Leonard, a famous author and the owner of an automobile, had villainously refused to part with this sum, he told her he had a hundred dollars of his own saved up and she was welcome to it.

He was sent out of the kitchen amid great rejoicing and returned with a bright twenty-five-centavo piece.

There was nothing for Maria to do but come to the villainous and wealthy Senhor Leonard and tell him officially what he knew already—that she needed three dollars for eggs.

She came in with a preparatory sob or two, her pretty face quite dark with grief and her black curly hair suitably disarrayed with the sorrow of poverty. I was pretending to read a copy of the London *Times* which I had bought for ten cents after a considerable wrestle with my conscience over the expense.

"Senhor Leonard," said Maria when she had controlled the sobs sufficiently to speak, "the man wishes the money for the eggs. He is saying scandalous things about me in the village. It is three dollars only, senhor. Here, I will show you the full account." She came forward with a scrap of pink butcher's paper on which she had laboriously written out the egg account to show that we did indeed owe three dollars (seventy-seven escudos) for eggs.

"You have had forty dollars this week for groceries, including eggs," I said. "I have no more money for you."

"Forty dollars is not enough," said Maria. "Senhor Leonard, I call upon the good Lord to witness that for forty dollars it is impossible in Portugal to buy meat and fish and potatoes—potatoes are like gold in the market now—and bread and eggs and vegetables for us all. The prices go up every week. In the houses in the village people weep at nights because of the way prices are going up, and those who have little babies are sorry they are born."

"You had forty dollars," I said. "There is no more."

Maria withdrew in a flood of tears, turning several times before she reached the door to implore me to relent. But in a battle at which the stakes are the survival of my own family or Maria's retention of the affections of her handsome husband, I could be as hard as Shylock. I would not part with the three dollars.

The next day Maria was sick. I must state honestly that she was really sick, and I called the doctor to treat her. But I felt that the sickness was to an extent self-induced, and that she wished, by falling sick, to demonstrate to us how important it was to keep her well and happy, so that she could perform the important service of going to the market for us.

I do not believe it entered her head that we would ever do the marketing ourselves. For when I announced that I would go to the market myself and buy the needed vegetables and food, she was dismayed. She made an attempt to dissuade me, assuring me that I would be cheated. But I said I would market carefully, and then she begged me to buy fish at such and such a stall, meat at another, and vegetables at such and such a place where I would get honest value and not be robbed. She gave me a note with these places listed and I took it and determined that these were the last people I would approach to buy food.

When I got to the market all my worst suspicions concerning Maria were proved to the hilt. Good cuts of meat, she assured us, legs of lamb or chops or steaks, were out of the question. They were so expensive that nobody could afford them. At the butcher's I bought a beautiful leg of lamb at twenty cents a pound. Potatoes (worth their weight in gold) turned out to cost three cents a pound. Wonderful vegetables, which Maria had assured us could be purchased only at impossible prices, were to be had for next to nothing. And the same went for fish.

In short, I did the marketing for the household for three days for about four dollars, buying many extras, such as bananas and jam. Twenty dollars a week, then, would be quite ample for grocery money and Maria had been getting forty. No wonder she could afford to buy the beautiful jacket and the mattress and the bicycle for her husband, agreeing to pay two dollars a week perhaps for each purchase.

I returned home determined that as soon as Maria was well, I would cut her allowance for groceries down to twenty-five dollars a week. If she did not like it, she could seek employment elsewhere.

It was Hazel who persuaded me differently. She did it wisely, as a woman should, by keeping silent. When I told her again and again that from here on Maria would get only twenty-five dollars a week and she merely nodded and looked troubled, I began to think the matter over.

It was important for Maria to keep her young and handsome husband. She loved him desperately and she was eight years older than he—a terrible gulf in Portugal. At the fiestas in the village he stood out like a smiling god among the other men, and the women laughed closely in his face and lit his cigarettes and brought him wine.

To keep this man she had to buy him things. She was not dishonest; stealing for the sake of storing up money. The money she stole, if "stole" is indeed the right word, she spent generously on Marco. She stole for love then, for the great love of her life, that this love might never leave her. It lay in my power to wreck all this and who was I, with my prim principles concerning honesty, to make Maria desperately unhappy and render more precarious a life and a union already full of anxieties?

When Maria had recovered, I told Hazel that I would continue to give her forty dollars a week. Hazel rushed out and told Maria and Maria came in, smiling like a child, with a pot of tea for me.

The next day the mailman was early and he had a letter for me. It was from my agent and he stood by while I opened it. Maria and Celita came out of the kitchen, for they knew the Senhor was expecting news of his book.

I opened the letter and out of the page leaped the wonderful word "Accepted."

"Hurray," I shouted, "we sold the book." The mailman beamed as if he himself had had a hand in this joyous event. I made a note to buy him a new tire for his motor bicycle. Maria swept Arabella up in her arms and nearly crushed her with joy and love.

I looked a little further in the envelope and found a check for three hundred dollars. A Swiss Reading Society had, out of the blue sky, bought some kind of rights for one of my previous books.

I took Hazel out to a lobster dinner at a fashionable restaurant on the beach at Guincho.

We borrowed the money from Maria.

10.

ONE MORNING, WHILE I WAS still abed, I heard in the thin, clear mountain air a wavering cry which ended with an abrupt staccato note and then was repeated again and again. I had never heard such a cry before and lay for a while listening to it. Plainly it was made by a man. It had a sort of oriental nuance to it, like the cry of the Muezzin summoning the faithful to prayer.

It was a beautiful day. Out of the window I could see huge white clouds, soft and expanding, rolling majestically across a sky of deep blue. The sun appeared and gently disappeared, and I knew that on the mountain opposite the house, in the tiny fields cleared from the forests, there would be a procession of cloud shadow over the ground—a wonderful display of forms, ever changing in shape and density and moving across the ground.

I got up and at breakfast asked Maria who was making the strange sound.

"The men are plowing," she said. "They are talking to their oxen. That is the way one talks to an ox all over the world."

I finished breakfast quickly and, taking Kevin, went out to see this wonder—a man talking to an ox. The man was in a field on the mountainside across the valley. In the clear air he was perfectly outlined against the brownish earth on which he stood, as sharp as a figure in an etching. He had a plow and two oxen yoked to it. The oxen had long, graceful horns, which appeared as beautiful curved lines even at that distance. The man wore a stocking cap with a bobble at the end of it. It hung down over one side of his face. I could see him jerk the plow up out of the ground and then we heard, with exquisite clarity, the plaintive cry with the staccato stop on a high note. Slowly the oxen leaned forward on the yoke; slowly they put one big and yet graceful foot in front of the other; slowly the plow moved. And as ox and plow moved laboriously forward, the man repeated his wavering cry, at once a plea, a command, and a complaint that the oxen and himself should be so harnessed to the ground and made to earn their bread in this manner.

I was enchanted, and with Kevin raced down our side of the mountain and across the little road and river at the bottom and up the other flank of the mountain to the field in which the man was plowing. He came slowly along the field toward us, stopping, it seemed, every minute to jerk the plow up out of the furrow, clear off the share some root or clump of tangled grass, and then continue.

When he drew near he looked at us out of a blank mahogany face; like the Spirit of the Ages might look upon mere mortals, with patience and sorrow. Then he took off his stocking cap and bowed with a beautiful gesture and said, *"Bom dia, senhor."*

"Bom dia, senhor," I replied, for I had now been long enough in Portugal to appreciate the deep politeness of the Portuguese. The meanest beggar you meet in the meanest street is "senhor" which may roughly be translated as "gentleman." To inquire the way you do not say, "Can you tell me the road to Lisbon?" but, "Can the gentleman (or the lady) tell me the road to Lisbon?"

I had by now sufficient Portuguese to ask the plowman what words he spoke to his oxen and whether he guided them only by words. He explained that the oxen did not understand Portuguese, but there was a kind of oxen language in which they were well versed. This language was a language of sound only—a glissando of the voice through a series of quarter notes which the oxen all over Portugal understood. One learned it only by listening to it. He had learned it from his father, who had gotten it from his father, and so on.

"Can the gentleman tell me how long this language of the oxen has been spoken in Portugal?"

The plowman reflected.

It was *muito antiqua*—it has always been so. Then I began to realize that here was one of the most ancient agricultural cries in the world. Perhaps it was a thousand or two thousand years old, this cry. It was a cry which Vasco da Gama, should he return to Portugal, would recognize immediately. No doubt it had been a dear and familiar sound to him and he had thought of it often during his splendid voyage into the unknown.

The plowman had with him a long, slim pole like a fishing pole. This was his other means of communicating with his oxen. When he put it in front of them, they stopped. When he touched them on a horn with it, they turned to the side touched.

Might I examine his plow?

Certainly. He jerked it out of the four-inch furrow which it had made in the ground and again I realized I was in the presence of something incredibly old. For the plow was of the exact same design one sees in drawings of the plows of Saxons of the sixth and seventh centuries. It was little more than a pointed piece of wood, like the nose of a shark, which carved a furrow in the ground, one single furrow, when pulled by the huge oxen. There was not even a wheel on this plow. There was a screw by which the depth of the furrow could be regulated. This screw was not of metal, but beautifully carved out of a piece of olivewood. It was then a screw such as Archimedes must have whittled centuries before the birth of Christ.

I should have been more respectful in the presence of such an ancient instrument, the prototype of all the plows ever developed by man and one of which some examples are to be seen in the wall paintings in Egyptian tombs. But I was from the New World, and brash.

"Would not the gentleman's work be easier," I inquired, "if he used a metal plow with several shares and had it pulled by a machine?"

He smiled at me patiently. He explained he had heard of such plows though he had never seen one. But they would be of no use to him. His farm was small and all the fields small—the largest no bigger than three acres. If he used such a plow his field would be plowed in less than an hour.

"And, senhor," he concluded, "what would I do with the time saved? I will plow this field with my oxen in two days. On the third day I will sow the grain. It is no benefit to me if the grain is sowed two days earlier. Wheat will not be hurried but will take its time. It knows when to sprout and when to come into ear, and two days do not matter to wheat."

I realized how foolish I had been to ask the question but he had not quite finished with his rebuke.

"And if I used one of these machines, into which one must put expensive fuel, what would become of my oxen? There must be work for oxen to do."

Certainly there must be work for oxen to do. Through the ages they have served man, patient companions of his labor in the cold and the heat and the wind and the rain. They are not to be discarded because man has become too clever for them.

It was the turn of the plowman to ask a question.

"The gentleman is from England?"

The mistake was natural, for the English go frequently to Portugal, as yet largely undiscovered by Americans.

"No," I said, "from America. From California."

"It is a beautiful place, no doubt."

"Yes. It is very sunny. There are lots of orange trees. People live well." But I could not tell him much about California. We had not sufficient terms of reference in common. How could I describe to this man, for instance, a city such as Los Angeles, which has had to build eight-lane highways over its houses because the original streets below cannot cope with the traffic? These things are so ridiculous as to be unbelievable.

"You like Portugal?"

"Yes," I said.

There was a little twinkle in his eyes. "Because of the oxen and the plow?"

And I realized indeed that this was one reason why Portugal had been beckoning me and why in the supermarket in California I had always wound up looking at the little cans of fish with the word "Portugal" on them. Because Portugal is not only a different country from America, but it exists in a different time from the twentieth century. In going to Portugal one travels not only in space but in time. One travels to a new place and one travels back through the centuries to a very ancient culture which makes a mockery of the scurrying taxis and busses of Lisbon and Porto.

Portugal is the tenth century and the twelfth and the fifteenth. These centuries are more real in Portugal than the twentieth century and the modern highways. The highways (excellent highways for so small a country) and the trains and the modern hotels are all intruders. Portugal reached its fruition in the fiteenth century and basically it has not gone forward since then.

"How did you know it was the oxen and the plow?" I asked.

"Because you came running to look at them, senhor, like a man running to his home."

He turned to the oxen and cried to them in their language, and the sound made the muscles of my neck and shoulders stiffen. They turned slowly around on their splayed feet and the plowman adjusted the plowshare.

"The gentleman should look at the windmill," he said. "He will like it as much as the plow," and he went on with his work.

I went up to the windmill. It stood atop a stone knoll and I had often seen it from across the valley. As a matter of fact, I could judge the weather by it. When the sails were pointed toward our house, the day would be fair. But when they were set to point toward the incoming tide of wind from the Atlantic, we knew we were in for heavy rain and sometimes hailstorms. I went up to the windmill with the curious feeling that I was walking back through time three hundred or more years. If a man in the trunk hose of the fourteen hundreds had greeted me at its tiny door, I would not have been in the slightest bit surprised.

The windmill was a truncated cone, built of limestone, plastered on the outside and limewashed. It had four sails and they were real sails.

In Holland the sails of the windmill are made of wood slats. But the Portuguese are a seafaring nation and on their windmills they use the jib sails of a boat. The sails were rigged as the sails of a ship are rigged—with a stay along the luff and a sheet to make the corner of the leech fast to the pole which it drove by revolving the axis of the mill.

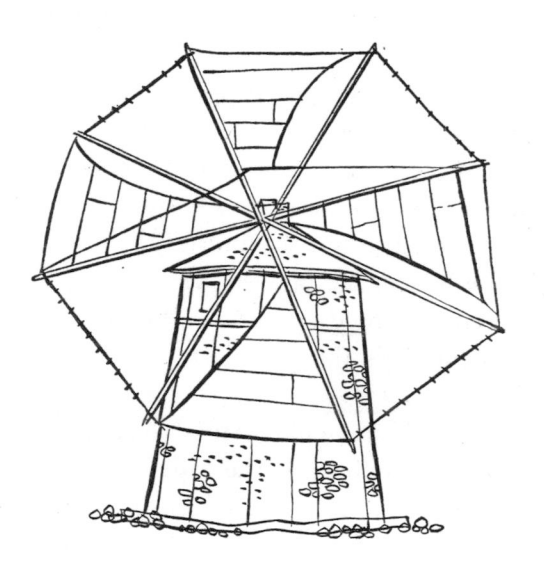

How very natural that the Portuguese, knowing a sail will drive a ship through the water, should know also that the same sail will turn the axle of the windmill, and should trust a sail of canvas rather than any contraption of wooden slats.

The mill was working at the time, and a wonderful variety of whistles formed an accompaniment to the work. For a while I was at a loss to discover where these beautifully tuned whistling noises came from. Then I noticed that on the stay or rope that connected the ends of the four poles or masts forming the arms of the windmill, on which the sails were set, there were little clay pots of different sizes.

These were the whistles.

The big ones gave out a beautiful, deep, fluid note. The small ones were like a piccolo. The whole effect was of an ensemble of woodwinds, from perhaps bassoon through clarinet to piccolo, piping away while the windmill worked.

That, I also learned, was a trait of the Portuguese. A cheerful people, they delight in toys and see no harm to having toys, like these whistles, worked by such necessary tools as windmills. Where else in the workaday world would one find anything so enchanting?

We went inside. It was dark, for the door was so tiny that we blocked all the light normally admitted by it. There was one tiny window high up, and when our eyes were accustomed to the gloom, though I should have been prepared for what I saw, it yet surprised me.

A windmill is operated, in simple terms, by a drive shaft, which is turned when the sails revolve. This drive shaft, through a simple gear, turns another shaft which is set into a heavy circular stone. The stone revolves atop another, which is stationary. Grain poured between the two stones is thus ground to flour.

The windmill which I was inspecting was operated by this classic method. But there was one almost incredible difference.

The gears were all of wood. The cogs were of wood and their wooden teeth mesh in pinions of wood. There was not a piece of metal used anywhere. The Iron Age had not yet reached this windmill and the men who made it.

Since the power of a windmill depends to some extent on

the force of the wind, there must be some method of con-
trolling this force so as to regulate the speed at which the
grinding stone moves. There was such a provision in this windmill—a number of gears operating on much the same principle
as the gears in an automobile gearbox.

All these gears were of wood.

For centuries, then, before the discovery of the means of
working metal by machinery, and so making steel cogs and
pinions, the Portuguese had made their machinery out of
wood, as had the rest of the world. The rest of the world had
long since turned to metal. But Portugal clung to the older
method of the craftsman, and olivewood is still an efficient
substitute for steel in the windmills of Portugal.

Once again I was struck by the thought of all those great
figures of the Middle Ages and the early Renaissance years
who would have been perfectly at home in such a windmill as
this. Had not Rubens in his youth been employed in a windmill? I fancy I have read that this was so.

We went out into the sunlight in silence, and from the top
of the stony knoll on which the windmill was situated looked
over the roofs and little crooked back streets of the village of
Malveira da Serra. The village, when I first caught sight of it,
had seemed oddly familiar, as if I had been there some time
before. The little lanes between chest-high stone walls, the
red-tiled roofs of the houses—five or six or even eight roofs to
a house, all at different angles and few of them more than six
feet from the ground—awoke some memory in me.

On these roofs, pumpkins were ripening in the sun and white
pigeons waddled and pouted, or wheeled over them in flutter-
ing splashes of light. Attached to each house were stables for
donkeys or cattle or oxen, and cats slept in the discarded

bracken while one or two hardy flies (for this was December) buzzed sleepily about. Little children, ragged but healthy, played among the cats and the donkeys, and their granddames sat with shawls over their heads, knitting or taking the sun.

Certainly it was all familiar. But where had I seen it before?

The ancient cry of the plowman came to me across the fields and the little whistles on the windmill twittered above my head and a dog dashed after a hen that disappeared in a flurry of squawks and feathers.

And suddenly I knew where I had seen it all before. It was in the paintings of Breughel and Rubens and a dozen other Renaissance painters. I found myself there in The Europe of the Renaissance. It was not a stage setting that surrounded me but the real substance. The lanes with the chest-high walls— those were the places where swords had flashed and the blood of dying men had mingled with the mud while their prayers for the salvation of their souls fell upon the dark night air.

The mean tavern at the corner was the place where the traveler knocked after sunset, and was eyed fearfully through a little wooden shutter that opened in the stout door. And the barnyard strewn with bracken and cats and old women—there are a thousand paintings of such barnyards with cats and women, and pumpkins ripening on the roof, and white pigeons circling in the air, all of them three hundred years old.

I had slipped out of the twentieth century into the fifteenth. It was enchantment, and yet it was true. This was the Portugal that unknowingly, drawn by some deep instinct, I had set out to find.

11.

IT GOES WITHOUT SAYING THAT anyone who judges a country on its cooking is a plain vulgarian, and yet it would be a disservice to the public at large to pretend that Portuguese cooking is anything but wretched.

To be sure there are many excellent foreign restaurants in Lisbon where you may have the best cuisine at very modest cost. And outside of Lisbon, on the beach at Guincho, there are little restaurants specializing in sea foods where the lobster and crab are worthy both of appetite and respect.

But the plain cooking of Portugal, since one cannot spend all one's time dining out, is an offense to the palate and the stomach. It makes of each meal a duty which must somehow be endured. You drag yourself to the table, and the very thought of the dinner which awaits you destroys what appetite you may have had.

It is not just that the Portuguese cannot cook well. Their talent lies in the opposite direction. They can cook worse than any other nation of my acquaintance. They have a positive genius for ruining foods, and the only answer, for anyone intending to live in Portugal for any length of time, is to train your own cook personally.

We early discovered this with Maria. She was very willing to learn, and not at all prejudiced against non-Portuguese methods of cooking. She was anxious to please and we were anxious that she should not be discouraged in her attempts.

The result was that we would praise something which in California we would have consigned to the sink, thanking God for garbage disposals.

Maria's staple soup was compounded of turnips and potatoes cooked in a little water to which had been added a generous helping of both olive oil and garlic. The average American has no idea how terrible hot olive oil tastes, and it is quite beyond my ability to describe the taste. But when to hot olive oil (slightly rancid to start with, as is most olive oil in Portugal) has been added a generous squeezing of garlic juice, the result is horrendous. This we got at lunch and dinner for several days while I searched around in all the Portuguese guidebooks we had to find the word for garlic. We desperately needed to tell Maria not to put garlic in the soup but I could not find the Portuguese equivalent.

Eventually I called the Irish consulate.

The conversation went something like this.

Myself: "I'm an Irishman, and I'm here from America with my family."

Voice of consulate: "That's interesting now. And is your wife from Ireland, too?"

"No. We live in California but she's from Arizona."

"Well, I was never in Arizona myself. I hear it's a very hot place."

"It is indeed . . . But . . ."

"Your wife could claim Irish citizenship if she wished by virtue of her marriage to you. Tell me, have you ever voted in an American election? That might have something to do with your status."

"No. I never voted because I'm not an American citizen. I'm an Irishman. My wife votes but she gets confused and asks me how to vote and I advise her. I suppose that's all right."

"Sure it is. I don't blame her at all. I hear that it's very confusing indeed the way they set up the ballots. You can't tell whether you're electing a judge or a hangman."

"Well, it wasn't about that that I wanted to call you. It's about the cooking here."

"Ah, you'll have a terrible time of it until your stomach's settled down. There's a kind of a stomach powder . . ."

"Yes, I know. I've eaten about a peck of it. It tastes like dried-up tooth paste and sits around glumly in your insides looking at all the work that's to be done. It's about soup. My cook makes soup with turnips and potatoes and olive oil and garlic. What's the Portuguese word for garlic?"

"*Alho.*"

"*Alho?*"

"That's right. Just say '*Noa gusto alho,*' and the whole world will be brighter for you."

"Gee . . . thanks. Thanks very much."

"Don't mention it at all."

I don't know about the consular service of other countries, but as far as I'm concerned you can't beat Irish consulates anywhere. They have the one essential that most others seem to lack—they realize that they're dealing with human beings who have not yet been reduced to mere statistics. At least that's my experience.

Primed by the Irish consulate in Lisbon, I went to Maria.

"*Bom dia,* Maria," I said, for one must always be polite.

"*Bom dia,* Senhor Leonardo," she replied, and her dark face blushed a slight pink because the Senhor had come into her kitchen, which made it something of a state occasion.

"Maria," I said, "Senhor Leonardo *noa gusto alho.* Maria *noa pode alho en sopa.*"

(The above isn't Portuguese. It's pidgin Portuguese, but it is what got me by in Portugal.)

"The Senhor does not like garlic?" said Maria incredulously.

"No," I said.

"Impossible," said Maria. "The children love garlic. When they come into the kitchen I make soup for them—stale bread, hot water, olive oil, and garlic. *Muito gusto.*"

I now realized why it was that the children reeked of garlic all the time.

But I stuck to my point. "No garlic in the soup, Maria, please," I said. And realizing that having gone this far, nothing I said hereafter could shock her further, I continued, "No garlic in anything. No garlic in scrambled eggs. No garlic in fish. No garlic in butter. No garlic in bacon. No garlic anywhere. Thank you very much." Then I walked out firmly.

That night Maria served her usual potato-and-turnip soup. She put it on the table with some trepidation and did not withdraw immediately, as was her custom. I ladled a plateful for each of the children and we said grace. Maria, standing in a corner of the dining room, said grace very loudly and fervently, petitioning Heaven, I believe, that the soup would not be rejected.

It is not my custom to taste things first when I have a large family who can perform this experiment for me. I therefore waited while Christopher ladled a spoonful of soup into his mouth.

"*Bom*," he cried. "*Muito bom!*"

This, however, was not a test, for Christopher has no sense of taste. He's a little animal and eats anything.

I turned to Kevin, who is more reliable. "Boy," I said, "drink some of that soup."

He took a little in a spoon and put it cautiously in his mouth.

Out of the corner of my eye I saw Maria in agonies of anxiety, twisting a napkin in her strong hands to relieve her nerves.

"Well," I demanded, "*bom* or no blinking *bom?*"

"*Bom,*" he said with such enthusiasm that I fancied it a little overdone. I recalled that Kevin is not past getting a revenge for parental disciplines by encouraging me to eat heartily of some foul dish, and I turned to Hazel.

"You try it," I said.

Hazel took a spoonful, swallowed it, and looked at me with surprise.

"*Bom,*" she said.

Since Hazel is incapable of acting any kind of part I was encouraged to try some myself. I put a spoonful in my mouth and it was delicious—potatoes, turnips, and rancid olive oil; not a trace of garlic.

"*Magnifico!*" I cried. "*Muito bom,*" and Maria went from the room in transports of joy.

From that day on, in her anxiety to learn how to cook to please us, she would stand in the corner until we had all tasted whatever dish she put before us. Then she would ask in a voice tight with apprehension:

"*Bom or noa bom?*"

The phrase became the key and theme of all our days in Portugal. Everything was either "*bom*" or "*noa bom.*"

Unfortunately the children, in their sympathy for Maria, whenever she put the question, would yell "*bom*" at the top of their voices and drive this home by adding "*gusto muito*" (I like it very much). This resulted in our getting day after day, *ad nauseam*, the same dish until it was necessary to tell Maria that she must change the menu.

We had a full week of the turnip-and-potato soup with the rancid and hot olive oil for lunch and dinner before I silenced the children and told Maria that we must have a change of menu. She hated to change the menu. Having found something that we liked, it seemed the height of folly to start serving something different which we might not like. Only firm insistence produced another kind of soup, *caldo verde*, which is some kind of shredded green vegetable cooked in a broth.

The Portuguese are not great meat eaters. Their staple is fish, and among the lower classes meat is probably not eaten more than once or twice a year, because in their terms it is expensive. Consequently, they have no idea how to cook meat. They tackle it in the same manner as fish—cooking it in rancid olive oil, or, occasionally, rancid butter.

Portuguese fish is excellent. The linguada, or sole, is magnificent and not to be equaled anywhere I know. Shrimps are perfection, as are other shellfish, and red mullet and halibut and other delights are served frequently. However, my family can tolerate fish but once a week and then only in a state of penance.

So it was necessary to convey to Maria that she must not serve fish for lunch and then fish for dinner, nor must she serve fish more than twice a week, and that on Tuesdays and Fridays.

Hazel, after much travail—I could not get her to call the American consulate for the information—finally discovered the words for "meat" and "potatoes" and how to divide meat into beef, veal, lamb, and pork. She also learned how to ask for "boiled potatoes," "mashed potatoes," and "French-fried" potatoes. Armed with this treasure, she took Maria aside and detailed the kind of menu we wished for each day of the week.

It did no good.

This was in the days when Maria was saving up for Marco's

fur-collared jacket, his new bicycle, and her inner-spring mattress. Maria was not going to spend money so badly needed for these essentials on meat for my family.

She came around only when I refused to eat fish dinners. I would inquire what was for dinner, and if informed that it was fish, would tell her that I was not hungry that evening. This hurt her cruelly. For a while she sulked, and then she smoldered, and finally gave way. We got our meat menus, and although the meat was invariably cooked in the horrible olive oil, still it was meat.

Feast days were days of horror for us, however.

The first to turn up was Thanksgiving, which we wished, as exiles from the United States, to celebrate nonetheless.

Portugal is a land in which men have considerably more stature than in the United States. Hazel might be mistress of the house but she was still a woman. But I, as master, was male and therefore infinitely more to be served and pleased and humored (as is proper, and thanks be to God for such essentially sound discrimination). Hazel, therefore, enlisted my aid in getting Maria to cook a turkey dinner for us for Thanksgiving.

I first explained to Maria that in America we had a day which was called the Day of Thanks Be to God and that this day celebrated the American colonists' survival of the hardships of their first winter in their new land. I don't know whether Maria got all this, for it is quite impossible to convince many Europeans that Americans have ever had to survive any sort of hardship. A common belief is that the early colonists arrived to find Automats and a plenitude of food awaiting them. Anyway, I did get over the idea that we were approaching the Fiesta da Obrigado a Deus, and it was therefore necessary for us to cook and eat a turkey.

At this point Maria balked. In Portugal turkeys (called *perus*) are eaten only at Christmas. No turkeys would be fat enough to be eaten at Thanksgiving. Furthermore, perus cost a great deal of money. Would the Senhor not settle for a fine sole which she could get cheap in the market?

I told her pretty sternly that if I served a fried sole for Thanksgiving dinner there was a strong possibility of my permit to re-enter the United States being canceled on the grounds of conduct unbecoming a gentleman. We must have a peru, and it was up to her to find one.

We haggled about it for a while. No perus were to be had, it seemed, for many miles.

This was not so, I pointed out. The forester at the bottom of the road had a barnyard full of perus who invariably chased the children when we went by.

Ah, said Maria, this was indeed true. But the forester was a man of great importance, though he received only a small salary. Therefore he was obliged to raise perus which he sold at Christmas time in Lisbon. He got a very good price for them and would insist upon such a price now. It would be an act of madness to buy a peru, not yet fully grown, for the inflated price which the bird would command on the Christmas market.

That, I insisted, was not a matter of primary consideration. I was not going to put off my family's celebration of Thanksgiving merely because perus were hard to get in Portugal. Maria must get a peru and that was all there was to it.

The peru, she insisted, would cost a fabulous price.

How much?

A medium-sized peru would cost a hundred escudos (four dollars, approximately).

Then, said I grandly, get us a medium-sized peru.

Once the bird was bought, it was released in a pen in the back yard, where Christopher promptly fell in love with it. He would sneak off to the pen and walk up to the turkey (a hen) which was quite tame, stroke its feathers, and talk with it. He came to me, thanked me for having bought him a playmate, and said he had always secretly wanted a turkey for a pet.

This posed another problem. It's a pretty harsh world in which a father has to butcher his son's playmate and serve it roasted to him for dinner in order to render thanks to God. Such a state of affairs goes beyond cannibalism, for cannibals hardly sit down to a feast of thanksgiving at which a bosom buddy provides the main dish. I consulted with Hazel, who is very wise in these matters, and she produced an admirably simple solution.

"We'll have to buy another turkey," she said.

"Supposing Christopher, or maybe Kevin or Patricia, falls in love with the second turkey?" I countered.

"We'll have to keep it separate where they will never see it," replied Hazel. "We'll arrange for someone in the village to keep it and the children won't know of its existence until it is put in front of them, golden brown and suitably stuffed, on the dining-room table."

I will skip the astonishment with which Maria received the news that we would have to buy a second turkey because the first had become a special friend of Christopher. She made an effort to convince me that we had already purchased the last available turkey in Portugal, but I was firm in insisting that another could be found somewhere. Finally she said she would see what she could do.

Knowing Maria's limitations as a cook, I undertook to instruct her in preparing the turkey and the manner in which it should be cooked. I explained about stuffing, and she delighted me with the assurance that she well knew how to stuff a bird, having learned this art from a French lady for whom she had worked and who had rented the house some time previously.

I then told her the quite simple procedure for roasting a turkey, stressing that it must be frequently basted so that the skin became a golden brown and did not dry out. To all this she nodded vigorously.

Finally Thanksgiving Day and Thanksgiving dinner arrived. From the kitchen there came a most appetizing smell of roast turkey mingling with the softer and more graceful odors of creamed cauliflower, whipped potatoes, warm rolls, and a tureen of green peas. All of these have their own subtle aromas readily distinguishable if the appetite is sufficiently sharp. The table had been covered with a beautiful snowy cloth of good damask, the glasses were polished to look like crystal, Tomaso, the gardener, with much bowing and pulling off of his beret, had produced a generous display of tawny chrysanthemums as rich in color as a good port wine. Celita had found a tiny American flag which stood proudly upon the table, as brave a standard, I thought at that moment, as was ever raised. We got through the soup without much ceremony and the children's cries of *"Bom, gusto muito"* brought a blush of pleasure to Maria's face.

But this was as nothing compared with the sparkle in her eyes, the furious blushing both from nervousness and delight, with which she brought in the turkey. I declare I have never seen a better-looking bird in all my days. It was trussed in the most handsome fashion, the breast thrust properly forth, the legs well secured over skewers in a manner which would have done credit to a poultry chef.

From the children there were, first, gasps of admiration, and then silence. I picked up the carving knife and made it ring agains the steel with that cheery, brisk flourish which is part of the pleasure of a good meal. Then I thrust the fork firmly into the bird and was immediately overcome with horror.

For out of the holes made by the fork gushed a stream of pinkish blood.

"What's the matter?" asked Hazel, who readily read disaster in my face.

"This turkey," I said, "is raw. The skin is cooked. The rest of it is hot, raw turkey."

Hazel looked at Maria. Maria sensed that something terrible was wrong—that on this extremely important occasion, in the presence of and with the knowledge of the whole household, she had failed miserably in her greatest effort.

Hazel (assuring her place in heaven if there is any justice at all) addressed the children.

"The turkey's raw," she said. "But you are all of you going to eat it just as if it was wonderful; as if it was cooked just as well as it could be. You"—she said, turning to me—"smile at Maria and tell her that it's terrific."

"*Magnifico,*" I said, adding in what I trusted was Portuguese, "*Maria muito boa cosinheira.*"

"*Bom, bom,*" said the children, led by Christopher, who loves all of humanity. He got out of his chair, his little face beaming with good will, and kissed Maria, for Portuguese cook or Greek captain, Christopher will kiss anybody, such is the depth of his love for his fellow men and his desire that none should be hurt.

Patricia said, "*Bom, bom,*" too, but she bent her head and tears of disappointment flowed down her cheeks.

Maria, hugging the beaming Christopher, wanted to know why Patricia was crying.

"Because she is a girl," I said. "All girls cry when they are happy."

"*Quotodina poconina*," said Maria. The phrase I have never been able to translate accurately let alone spell. I think it means "the little darling." She swept Patricia up into her arms and they cried a little together, Maria the tears of triumph and release from anxiety, Patricia, the tears of disappointment bravely bedecked with a trembling smile.

We ate the raw turkey and the stuffing which was mashed potatoes made into a gruel by the addition of olive oil—rancid, of course.

When you have taken a bite or two, hot, raw turkey flesh isn't bad. I won't go so far as to say that it is a dish which will sweep the United States, but it can be stomached by anyone of fortitude.

Altogether it wasn't a bad Thanksgiving dinner, and I was very proud of my family. They had not used the Thanksgiving feast as an occasion for a surfeit of good foods. They had dined miserably but with every evidence of cheerfulness in order not to hurt a fellow human being.

It seemed to me there was a true Thanksgiving in this, which might be pleasing to their Creator. But I was secretly worried about the approach of Christmas.

12.

GRADUALLY WE WERE SETTLING
into Portugal, merging with its people and its customs. The
process was slow, gentle, and almost imperceptible.

We went through the first stage of being delighted with
everything and being hugely polite to everybody we met.
This led to the next stage, when some of the things which had
charmed us on arrival—the elaborately tiled frontage of the
houses, for example—began to repulse us, and when the polite
smiles on our faces became too tedious a mask to wear.

We stopped smiling and being so polite. And people
stopped being so formal with us.

Everybody relaxed, and we began to feel that we didn't
have to say that we loved *everything* we saw in Portugal. We
could talk about things we didn't like and people were still
friendly. We had, in short, been accepted to the extent that
any foreigner is accepted in any country—including the
United States. We were still foreigners or aliens. But we were
friends as well, and might be turned to, in a pinch, for help.

The first sign of this easier state of living, this acceptance
of us, came when Maria asked whether Kevin might accompany Marco and herself to a fiesta being held in the village.
I would have preferred it if she had invited us. But I suppose
she would have felt a little self-conscious, dancing and drinking wine and perhaps even smoking cigarettes in the presence
of the Senhor and the Senhora. She asked Kevin, however,

and we said we would gladly let him go on the understanding that he wasn't to drink any wine.

This was a necessary restriction, for children, particularly of the poorer classes (the phrase is unavoidable, there are poorer classes in Europe but they are not serfs), frequently drink the *vinho verde* or *vinho tinto* of Portugal. Maria assured us that Kevin would drink no vinho. She, herself, she continued, was most abstemious, as was the handsome Marco. Furthermore, she would see that Kevin got home at an early hour—midnight.

I said I'd call for Kevin at nine o'clock, and so I did. What went on at the fiesta I do not know, and from Kevin's account could not piece it out very well.

There was an orchestra, consisting mostly of brass instruments plus a few accordions and violins. There was unceasing dancing. Everybody, Kevin said, danced a lot and drank. Also they smoked cigarettes all the time. And there were a lot of children there.

The Portuguese have not discovered the American convenience of baby sitters. They take their children with them to their dances (fiestas, they call them, for everything is a fiesta). Infants wrapped in shawls are handed by mothers to their neighbors at the dance hall while Mother takes a whirl around the floor. They stay, the babies, until the fiesta breaks up, which is usually around dawn. But Portuguese children stay up to astonishing hours anyway. You may find them even in the wealthier homes still about at ten and eleven at night. The Portuguese, in our terms, spoil their children, refusing to discipline them to the extent of putting them to bed at, say, eight each evening.

In other ways, however, they do discipline them. The wealthier people live in terror of the sun. When they take

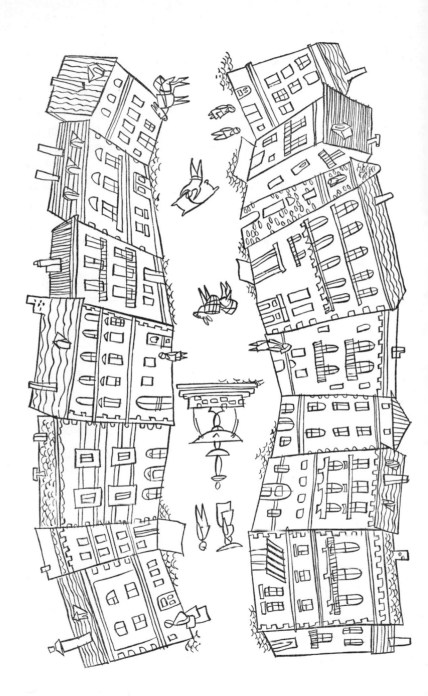

their children to the beach, the poor mites are dressed in their Sunday best, boys often with long stockings covering their knees. The children wear hats to protect them from the sun and parade along the boardwalk miserably scrubbed and in their best, looking with longing at the sand and the jolly, rolling sea in which they must not play lest they get tanned by the vicious sun.

I called, then, for Kevin at the fiesta at nine in the evening and took him home. Marco and Maria returned around five in the morning. She was up at seven, having almost literally danced all night, as bright as a sparrow.

"You do not feel tired, Maria?" I asked.

"No, senhor. I do not get tired at fiestas. Only through work."

But Marco was tired. He didn't go to work the following day and I suspected that he had a hangover. Maria, pressed, admitted that Marco did not feel too well.

"It is the cigarettes," she said stoutly. "One should not smoke so many cigarettes."

"Didn't Marco also drink some wine?" I asked.

"Oh, yes," said Maria. "Of course he drank a lot of wine. But wine does not hurt anyone. It is only the cigarettes which spoil his appetite and give him a headache."

Later, an elderly man living in a nearby village, who was a great drinker of wine, went berserk one day and shot his daughter and his grandson.

"Anyone could tell that that was going to happen," said Maria, when she had given us the news with great dramatic enjoyment. "He was always smoking cigarettes. They drove him out of his head."

The fiesta to which Maria and Marco invited me, and which was a milestone on the road to our acceptance in the village, was held in honor of a schoolteacher who had taught at the village school for a quarter of a century.

"Everybody loves the Senhora Professora," she said, "and the whole village will be there. They have planned a great farewell for her."

"I will not be intruding?" I inquired.

"Oh, no, senhor," said Maria. "All would be pleased if you would come to honor our schoolteacher."

I was profoundly moved and complimented by this, and went with Marco and Maria to the village school where the event was to take place. Marco, passing under an acacia in full bloom, plucked a sprig of golden blossoms from it and indicated that I should do the same. At a fiesta one wears flowers, even if male and bearded.

There was a large crowd in the road outside the school and in the schoolyard. There were women in their very best dresses made at home out of material bought after a great deal of heart searching over the expense. The women eyed each other shyly and proudly, with mutual assurances that they looked very well indeed. Their menfolk were likewise wearing their very best clothes. Their rough, thick-soled boots were shined to as high a polish as the leather would take. They wore, for the most part, blue-serge suits, carefully pressed and glossy from wear across the back of the coat and the seats of the pants. These men, laborers and farmers all of them, felt awkward in their suits and did not know what to do with their hands.

The hands with which they earned a living now became a nuisance to them in their Sunday suits. They hooked their thumbs in their jacket pockets, and their wives spoke sharply to them for spoiling the set of their jackets. They stood with their big hands clasped before them, but this seemed awkward, so they put their hands in their trouser pockets to get them out of the way, only to be told furiously by their wives not to ruin their trousers by doing such a thing.

They hitched at their belts, fingered their collars, and looked at the sky and the fields. Many of them stood over by the wall of the schoolyard and put their hands on it. But their anxious wives were soon after them, scolding them for leaning on the wall, and the men deserted it and stood huddled together, awkward and uncomfortable and unhappy but determined not to leave.

The children were likewise turned out in their best. Their faces had been scrubbed until they were shiny. The boys' hair was slicked down like black enamel over their skulls and the girls' hair was combed, brushed, and tied in bright bows. You could tell father and son readily by reference to the suits. The son wore an older suit of his father's, of the same pattern cut down.

But since the suit must last for a long time, it was invariably made too big on purpose so that the boy would grow into it. The boys looked even more uncomfortable than the sires. But they were not so quelled. A few of them started a game of tag in the schoolyard and soon they were all playing in it, ignoring the threats of their fathers and the screeching pleas of their mothers. Their sisters looked on, half-disdainful, half-envious. On such occasions a girl hardly knows whether it is better to be feminine and superior or masculine and have fun.

For the occasion the schoolhouse had been decorated with paper streamers and several flagpoles had been erected on the yard with its hard surface of adobe clay. The flagpoles had been set up with great care, with much thought given to deciding what flags they should bear. For such an important event the villagers realized that it was essential not to ignore or give offense to any nation. No allies of Portugal should be slighted by being unrepresented when the village of Malveira da Serra said farewell to its old schoolteacher.

On the big flagpole in the center of the schoolyard there were, naturally, the national colors of Portugal—a full-sized flag, bright and brave in the brisk mountain wind. This was flanked by flags of other nations. But since there was no money with which to purchase professionally made flags, the ladies of the village had made the flags themselves. This was a most difficult task, for in a village the size of Malveira da Serra no one could be found who was able to describe with accuracy the combination of colors and patterns making up the flags of other nations. Nor was there any library to which they could turn for information. The women were left to their own devices and did the best they could.

The tricolor of France was not too difficult—blue, white, and red in equal proportions. But Britain's Union Jack proved an impossible task. A flag consisting of the crosses of St. George, St. Andrew, St. David, and St. Patrick, combined with each other, was beyond their powers. The Union Jack bore a vague resemblance to that which existed in the time of the Stuarts. The Stars and Stripes consisted of six perpendicular red stripes on a white field with a blue union containing three stars in the lower far corner. Maria saw me looking at these flags and was embarrassed lest I should find fault with them, for she knew they were not correct.

But I did not find any fault at all. The flags might be wrong but the spirit was magnificent. It was important to the people of Malveira da Serra that the world should know that their teacher was retiring after forty years of teaching the people of the village. This was their way of achieving that, of paying at one and the same time a tribute to their teacher and a compliment to the allies of Portugal.

"*Bom or noa bom?*" asked Maria.

"*Bom,*" I replied. "*Muito bom,*" and I meant it.

Maria took me inside the school to show me the other preparations and especially to show me the farewell gift which the village had bought for the Senhora Professora.

This consisted of a massy silver salver and tureen, very heavy and beautifully embossed.

"Everyone gave money to buy these presents," Maria explained. Silver is not very expensive in Portugal. But these pieces, so elaborately worked, must have cost at least a hundred dollars—twenty-seven hundred escudos, which is a fantastic sum to raise in a village such as Malveira where a single dollar in a household represents a fair piece of capital.

Outside, the band had now arrived—the village band of brass instruments—and stood, dressed in blue uniforms, in the schoolyard. People were standing on top of walls and rocks looking expectantly down the road. There was a great crowd of people, and a hum went through it followed by a hush of expectancy as they spotted the car in which the Senhora Professora was riding coming up the steep hill to the school. There were three cars all together—one containing the Senhora Professora and two others with officials of the educational department of the Portuguese government. They had been shined to perfection and were decorated with white ribbons.

The Senhora got out—a tall, elderly, stooped woman dressed severely in black, and the people made a little path through which she could go to the school, and the band struck up some air quite strange to me. The band played very vigorously and importantly, and the people smiled, for they were proud of their band, which had a banner stating that it was "Fundidade in 1927" if I recall correctly.

When the band had finished, the aged teacher stood on the steps leading to the schoolhouse and made a speech.

Her voice was thin and tight with emotion, and at times she had the greatest difficulty continuing. The people who were gathered around had all at one time or another, I realized, been her pupils. She looked at the faces of men in their fifties and could recall the faces of boys not yet ten. She spoke of the pleasure she had had in teaching the children to read and to write and of the credit they were to her because they had learned these things. She said she would like to go on teaching but she was too old now to teach any more and they replied with a hum of "*noa, noa,* senhora." Some of the women in the crowd were weeping and some of the men rubbed their eyes with their fists and pretended that flies were bothering them.

There was one word that recurred in the address of the schoolteacher. It was "*saudade,*" which is one of the words of Portugal which cannot be translated accurately. It means sorrow and nostalgia, loneliness and yearning, acceptance of parting and yet grief at being parted. It means all those things and many more besides.

When the teacher had concluded, the crowd wished to make a reply. But the speech from the steps had seemingly been unrehearsed. It was not on the program of events and so no spokesman had been appointed from the village to reply to it. The villagers then took it upon themselves to make their own reply.

Someone started counting, and they all took it up. Like children reciting their multiplication tables, as all of them must have done many times before this bent and elderly woman, they counted.

"*Um, dois, tres, quartro, quinze, seize, sete,*" they chanted, showing her that they had learned this from her and had not forgotten it. It was easily the best kind of speech that could have been delivered for the occasion.

The rest of the event went off in a more formal manner, with tea and cakes and much shaking of hands, and then the Senhora Professora was driven away—out of Malveira and the school which had been the whole of her adult life.

Above, the funny little flags of the United States, Britain, and Portugal watched, and they could hardly have flown over a scene more fitting to the traditions of the people they represented.

13.

FOLLOWING OUR EXPERIENCE
with Thanksgiving dinner, we decided to be more prudent
about the Christmas feast and abjure turkey. The sensible
thing to do, it seemed to us, would be to buy a large ham for
the prime dish. There are excellent hams in Portugal, those of
Chaves in Tras os Montes being highly esteemed because the
pigs feed upon wild acorns which give their flesh a delicious
flavor. I inquired at the grocery in Cascais about a Chaves
ham but they were out of stock and so I settled on an American canned ham, which was enormously expensive, for there
is a huge import duty on all American produce to protect
Portugal's own produce. (As an example, matches in Portugal
are protected by a law requiring all Portuguese who own
cigarette lighters to take out a license for them, as for their
cars. Visitors, however, are allowed to bring in one cigarette
lighter for their own use. Bring in several and you are likely
to be in trouble.)

Hazel was anxious that Maria, Marco, Celita, and Tomaso
should have Christmas Day for themselves. She said that they
should all take two or three days off at Christmas time to enjoy
themselves and we would manage the household quite comfortably in their absence. But Maria would not hear of this.
She insisted that a certain minimum of work must be done by
the staff around the house, Christmas or no Christmas. To
reduce this work to the smallest amount, Hazel finally agreed

that Maria should heat the ham for Christmas dinner, which we would take about one in the afternoon. She would then have the rest of the day free, and to ensure their enjoyment, we gave them all an additional month's salary as a bonus.

They were enormously grateful for this, and diapers which Celita had left unwashed for some days were suddenly scrubbed and hung out on the line in the back of the house, where they got wetter, if that was possible, since it was raining with savage determination.

The first thing I had to do was get a Christmas tree. This meant securing the cooperation of the local forester, who wore a grey uniform of tunic and pants, a kepi, black leggings, and carried a beautiful little brass bugle slung on a baldric across his shoulders. He was the man from whom we had bought our Thanksgiving turkey. Maria passed the word to him that the Senhor was now in need of a Christmas tree, so he called at the house, courteous and jolly, armed with a huge double-bitted ax, and invited me to come into the forest to select my own tree. The pine forest about was government property, planted perhaps twenty years previously at the instigation of Dr. Salazar, dictator of Portugal. It was posted with stern notices warning everyone that it was forbidden to touch any of the trees or flowers of the forest. I felt as if I were defying a dictator in getting our Christmas tree, but since I had the forester on my side, and he a jolly man, I took comfort and courage from this.

We walked about a mile up a dirt road through the forest until we came to a small grove of pines. The forester plunged into it and displayed the trees, ruffling the young limbs as a saleswoman in a dress shop displays dresses on a rack.

I pointed to one or two which seemed good to me, but he shook his head. They would not do for the Senhor. He himself, a forester of great experience, would select a tree suitable to the Senhor. He selected one that would have made an excellent mainmast for a Cape Horn bark, but could by no other means than removal of the roof get into our living room. He was about to fell this with his double-bitted ax, ignoring my protests, when Tomaso, who had come along, took him aside and pointed to a smaller tree as more suitable. With a sigh of resignation, the forester felled this smaller tree with a few blows. I think for a long time he had been wanting to bring down a really big one. Twenty years he had been watching that forest, and in all that time had felled nothing but seedlings. He was a disappointed and frustrated man.

Now came the always-delicate problem of paying for the tree. How much? And how should this be done? Tomaso, with nice delicacy, withdrew some distance and I did a rapid calculation. The tree would have cost me five dollars in the United States. A hundred and fifty escudos, then, would be about right. But this was not America, so I produced a hundred-escudo bill for the forester.

He refused to accept it.

Was it too little, I wondered?

"You would make me very happy if you would take the money," I said. "After all, you have had to come away from your duties to get the tree for me."

"It has been a great pleasure, senhor," he replied, "but I cannot take the money for the tree."

There was a hint here of willingness to accept money, but not for the specific purpose of cutting down the government's trees. I began to understand. I eyed the silver bugle he carried, the kind of thing Robin Hood had used for hunting calls.

"Could the boy blow your trumpet?" I asked.

"Nothing would give me more pleasure, senhor," said the forester.

Kevin tried a couple of times and finally produced a horrendous note. The forester laughed and I gave him the bill which he now felt he could accept. There is a correct technique in all matters if one can only find it.

We got the tree back to the house and erected it in the dining room in a pot of sand. Maria, Marco, Celita, and Tomaso were delighted with it. They stood around it beaming at the lovely dark-green foliage, joined by Kevin, Patricia, Christopher, and Arabella, and the expression on the faces of the servants was quite as childlike as those of my children.

"*Bonita,*" they said. "*Bonita,*" and Maria giggled with delight and then blushed.

The next thing was the decorations. I expected some difficulty here but found none. The Portuguese have wonderful Christmas-tree decorations—not merely the usual strings of lights, but charming little brass lanterns with cellophane windows in red and green and orange which blink on and off very prettily. Then there are glass birds, wonderfully colored, with impossible tails and wings of silver bristles, and holy angels with impudent smiles upon their faces, and little glass animals, and so on.

The only thing they haven't got is the aluminum foil with which we in America cover Christmas trees to represent icicles. Hazel, however, had managed to sneak into our sixteen trunks some foil left over from the previous Christmas and some plastic icicles, and these brought gasps of admiration when we put them on.

It was a great moment when, the tree fully decorated, I inserted the main plug and the strings of colored bulbs, cunning little lanterns, lit up, flashing on the impudent angels flirting with the exquisite birds in the deep-green foliage.

"*Magnifico*," said Maria.

"*Bonita*," said Celita.

"*Bom*," said the children, dancing around, "*bom, bom, bom, bom, bom, bom.*"

The shy Tomaso was so overcome that all he could do was take off his beret and bow.

We had bought presents for everybody—a model of a DC-7 for Kevin, which ran along the floor flashing its lights; a six-shooter for Christopher who, having brought his Indians with him from California, was still engaged in repelling their attacks in the woods of Portugal; dolls for Patricia and for Arabella; and Hazel had made pretty aprons for Maria and Celita. Maria's, alas, was not quite finished, and she sulked

and pouted openly until it was done, when she was immediately all smiles and blushes, put it on, and went to show it
to Marco. I don't think Marco liked it, for Maria never wore
it again.

Christmas Eve we got the children to bed early and inquired of Maria whether she wished to go to midnight Mass
with us. She said she would but that her husband, Marco,
would not come because he did not believe in church going.

"This is true of all the men of Portugal," she said. "They
never go to church. They leave the women to pray for them.
It is a good job there are women, for without them no man
would enter heaven." I had in the past heard the opposite
point of view expressed, namely that but for women all men
had hopes of gaining paradise. However, I made no mention
of it.

We set out early for the Church of the Fishermen in
Cascais. It was a favorite church of mine, elaborately Portuguese with a paved court before it, shaded by trees, and atop
the façade of the building two little arches with a bell suspended in their centers. There is a large and slightly garish
painting behind the altar of Mary, Queen of the Sea, standing in a boat being beached by the fattest little rascals of
cherubs I have ever clapped eyes on. There is mischief in
every roll of fat, and two of them, pink and dimpled, look as
though they are more concerned with pushing each other out
of the boat into the water than bringing the Virgin ashore.
The subject of the painting is sacred but the rendering is
wonderfully human. The Virgin, while doing her best to look
lovely and holy, is obviously concerned about the fat little
cherubs either hurting each other or tipping her, halo and all,
into the water. In short, the whole picture is a delight.

Maria was right about the men. I had scarcely noticed it

before, but at least 90 per cent of the congregation were women, all in black, and all wearing as headdresses exquisite scarves of handmade lace. That elaboration which the Portuguese love was carried out in the interior of this church, which had gilded alcoves and statues and gracefully-curved altar rails. And yet it was plain that the church was a poor one. The gilding was worn, the statues chipped in places, and the pews old and bent askew. There was apparently not enough money to heat the place, for we shivered all through the service, though there was a blaze of light from a score of electric chandeliers.

The priest chose as his text these very chandeliers. It seems they were new and he did not like them, preferring candlelight, and he launched into a vigorous tirade, pointing out over and over again that electric lights were not necessary to Christmas. A poorer text for a Christmas sermon would be hard to find. But perhaps the priest, viewing the bulbs, each consuming expensive current, had in mind the plight of the poor of the parish. Anyway, he belabored the point for twenty minutes while the congregation shivered in the cold and the cherubs on the altar painting continued with their mischief.

When the service was over, we exchanged *"boas festas"* with a few of the congregation, and then drove home. All evening long, before the church service, we had been visited by cheerful little beggars, asking for money. They were accompanied by their mothers and were as fat as you could wish to see. Furthermore, I was entranced to notice that all the little girls, though they might be beggars, had gold rings in their ears, and surely, nowhere else in the world, do beggars appear at your door decorated in gold.

When we got back there was another group at the door.

Maria was angry and shooed them away with a stream of fierce reprimand that they should disturb the rest of the Senhor and Senhora with their whining outside his door at one in the morning. I do not believe they were really in want. All seemed most comfortably fed. But I take a different view of beggars from Maria, holding that if a man wishes to make a living by begging he has every right to do so, and is no more to be upbraided than someone who earns his money by any other means. So when Maria had shut the door firmly on this group and gone off to her own quarters, I scurried down the garden in the dark, caught up with the group, and gave them a little money, feeling like a conspirator and hoping that Maria would not find out.

I did ask them, however, to spread the word around to the rest of the mendicants that we were going to bed and would not like to be disturbed further that night. This seemed to be effective, for there were no more supplicants for alms that night.

On Christmas morning we were up early, awakened by the discharge of fireworks in the village. We found that all our careful instructions that the minimum of work was to be done around the house were being ignored. Celita, solid as an ox, was on her hands and knees in the dining room, polishing the floor, and I had almost to lift her up physically, expostulating that no work was to be done on the day of Christ's birth. I went out into the garden, and there was Tomaso grubbing away in the strawberry bed.

"No work today, Tomaso," I cried. "No work today."

"But I am paid to work today," said the faithful gardener.

"Well, quit and be damned to it!" I cried. "Come up to the house and drink a glass of wine." I led him blushing up to the kitchen where I assembled Maria and Marco and Celita and poured them each a glass of wine. Tomaso was so nervous that he spilled his down the front of his shirt, so I poured him another and fumbled for some cigarettes. I had none. Tomaso, still blushing furiously, reached in his worn shirt and took out a packet of little thin Portuguese cigarettes which sell for about four cents for twenty.

He offered them to me, enormously embarrassed at his own daring. I took one and lit it.

"*Bom*," I cried. "*Muito bom.*"

Tomaso was hugely pleased. The poor fellow had had nothing whatever to offer me. He could afford, I found, only three packets of these cigarettes a week. Now he gave me a whole packet of cigarettes. Whenever I met him in the garden after that he would bow and then offer me a cigarette. I fancy that in my acceptance of his little gift he had achieved some measure of emancipation. No man is without stature who has something to give another.

The day being properly started, we had a very light breakfast and the children set about opening their presents. And then, at one o'clock, came the main meal of the day.

We had asked for ham, and that is what we got.

Maria set the table and placed the large canned ham on a platter before me and nothing else. No potatoes, no peas, no gravy. Nothing but the ham, and that was only slightly warm.

That was too much for Hazel. "Where are the potatoes?" she demanded.

"The Senhora asked only for ham, no potatoes," said Maria. "Potatoes tonight for dinner."

"This is our dinner," said Hazel. "You are free for the rest of the day. It is not necessary for you to come back and cook dinner." Maria could not understand anybody eating the main meal in the middle of the day and going without dinner.

"We could have ham sandwiches," I said.

"Ham sandwiches for Christmas dinner?" stormed Hazel. "Whoever heard of anybody eating ham sandwiches for Christmas dinner?"

But that's what we had anyway. Maria did retreat to the kitchen and cook some French-fried potatoes. But the olive oil was a little more rancid than usual and the potatoes were somewhat raw so we settled for ham sandwiches and shooed her out of the house to visit her in-laws, with definite instructions that she was not to come back and cook for us any more that day. We were extremely grateful, for the peace that descended on the house, that there wasn't another feast day coming up until the Fourth of July.

As far as I am concerned, Christmas afternoon is meant for sleeping. Having assured myself that all the children had toys, I called them together, told them to play and enjoy themselves, warning them that the first one who got into a fight or started shouting would get spanked by Daddy, Christmas or no Christmas.

I then retired to the bedroom, and had just fallen asleep when there came, fortissimo through the window, a huge chord on several brass instruments, reinforced (though no reinforcement was necessary) by the clanging of cymbals, the striking of triangles, and the thunder of drums. For a second I lay there paralyzed, unable to account for this shattering noise, which continued with vigor, getting even more fortissimo. Hazel came running into the room, her face bright with excitement.

"The village band," she cried. "They've come to serenade us."

I could only just hear what she said above the din, and thought serenade the poorest word to apply to the perform-ance. Suddenly the brass fortissimo was replaced by a waver-ing diminuendo, screams of excitement and fright inter-mingled with the sharp barking of Tully.

The dog, as I noted before, has a fine ear for music and was as outraged by the band as I. Plainly he had charged into them, driven beyond all endurance.

Kevin now rushed into the room.

"Come quickly, Daddy," he said. "Tully has got the man with the drum cornered in the rosebushes." I dashed outside to find the village band scattered in panic all over the lawn. The drummer was indeed backed into the rosebushes, and using his drum as a shield, was trying to beat off Tully with his drumsticks. The more daring of his comrades were rally-ing to his rescue, hitting at Tully with trumpets, clarinets, and trombones, so that the dog was whirling and snapping and barking in a whirlpool of flashing instruments and a bedlam of assorted cries. I charged into this melee, collecting a swipe on the side of my head from a trombone and another on my shoulder from a drumstick, and grabbed Tully by the collar. He promptly pulled me off balance, and I knocked down a small man with a portable xylophone. He tumbled down a steep bank to an accompaniment of tinkling notes from his instrument. Tully was thoroughly aroused and could not be brought under control, for he was unable to hear me shouting at him, and my hand on his collar was just another unfriendly hand as far as he was concerned.

Eventually the bandsmen retreated far enough to let me get a good grip on the dog, and I bawled "TULLY" at him loud enough to be heard in Lisbon.

He immediately calmed down, and tucked his stub of a tail

between his legs and made for the house. But as he passed me
I could see a particular kind of grin on his ugly mug. He had,
in short, rarely had so much fun and had been granted the
one delight denied to most music critics—a direct physical
assault on the musicians, scattering them to the winds.

When I had him safely locked at the back of the house,
the band reassembled, and I first ascertained that none of them
had been hurt.

They then started their serenade again, but without the
bravura and fortissimo with which they had launched their
first effort. Tully, still unquelled, barked a few times from the
back of the house, and this was most distracting to the bandsmen. The more timid of them, at each bark, stopped blowing
and retreated a few paces from their fellows, so that the
music was at best ragged and uncertain.

Still, they went on, and when they had finished their first
piece, inquired whether the Senhor was from America. I replied that I was and that my wife was a native Norte Ameri-
cano. There was some consultation among the band, and two
men now came to the front carrying the orchestral banner—
the one which said that this was the orchestra of the village of
Malveira da Serra and that it was "Fundidade in 1927."

One held the flagpole, while the other, taking the end of the
banner farthest from the pole, held it outspread so that it could
be plainly seen. Then they launched into "The Star-Spangled
Banner" with such effect that it brought tears to Hazel's eyes
and I was by no means certain of my own self-control. When
they got to the parts about the "rockets' red glare" and
"bombs bursting in air" one of them let off half-a-dozen
homemade rockets. These hissed skyward and exploded with
a noise like fieldpieces—a remarkably dramatic touch with the

trumpets screaming and the man with the big drum thundering briskly away.

Altogether we were very pleased and complimented to have been serenaded by the village band and gave them two hundred escudos with which to celebrate their Christmas.

This was an error.

I had hoped to retire for my nap when they departed (after a glass of wine all around). But the word quickly spread that there was money to be had at our villa. And all that afternoon and evening and far into the night groups of villagers called upon us to sing some Christmas music. There seemed to be only one Christmas carol in that part of Portugal. It is called "Boas Festas." The tune is as undistinguished as a radio jingle, scarcely making use of half an octave, and the verses run to a score or more. We had this carol, "Boas Festas," until late at night from different groups, and ran out of money and had to borrow some from Maria, who seemed to have plenty.

Finally, to prevent the children's being constantly disturbed and to get a little privacy, we had to resort to a most un-Christian stratagem. We tied Tully down by the gate at the bottom of the garden. His fame had spread through the village, and we had no more carol singers that night.

Before we went to bed we remarked to Maria that much as we had enjoyed the caroling we were glad it was over.

"This is nothing," she said. "In Portugal the great feast is not Christmas but Twelfth Night, the sixth of January."

"On Twelfth Night," I replied, "you will tell everybody in the village that all here have measles."

Maria giggled. I don't know whether she did or not, but we had no visiting musicians on that day.

14.

EVERYBODY WAS WAITING FOR
Hazel to have her baby.

Kevin was waiting, Patricia was waiting, Christopher was waiting, Arabella was waiting, I was waiting, friends in America were waiting, and so also were Maria, Marco, Celita, and Tomaso. Every morning when she appeared for breakfast we would each (except Arabella, who didn't speak English but was learning Portuguese quite rapidly) ask Hazel how she felt.

"How do you feel?" we would say, putting into the word "feel" a special emphasis so that she would know we were not inquiring into any kind of foolishness such as having a headache or not having slept well.

And Hazel, to our disgust, would reply, "Swell."

That put a kind of gloom on the day for a while. We didn't want her to feel swell. We wanted her to have an exciting pain or two which would indicate surely that the long-awaited baby was due.

Maria would then shrug and look at me with some commiseration, and at Hazel with reproof as if she was merely being stubborn about the whole business by withholding deliberately the baby we all wanted to see.

"Gee," said Kevin, "I don't think I can wait until that baby comes. It's been the longest time coming."

"They all take nine months, more or less," I said. "You took nine months, too, you know."

"It's this rain," said Kevin. "I'll bet he's so snug in there he doesn't want to come out into this silly old rain."

The same thought had occurred to me because it had been raining for a week. When it rains in Portugal, it is like Ireland. The woes of the world descend in the form of water upon the land. The rain comes down white and hard, hammering the ground and rebounding in splashes like bomb bursts. The children had nothing to do and sat around eying their mother sullenly, wishing she would cheer things up for them by having the baby, which would be exciting. But Hazel seemed intent upon setting some kind of record for pregnancy, perhaps extending the period to eighteen months.

To take the pressure off her I racked my brains for some kind of game to amuse the children. They were tired of ticktacktoe, all except Arabella, who still couldn't figure out how to play it. I'd shopped for rainy-day games for them but could find none that were not noisy. I searched my own memories of such occasions. What had I done when I was bored as a boy and confined indoors? With what weapons had I warded off the waves of tedium which enveloped my mind when in class I was given some incomprehensible passage in Latin to translate?

The answer was paper airplanes.

I had made paper airplanes through the greater part of Caesar's campaign in Gaul and had used the same antidote during exercises in parsing sentences from Newman and Macaulay.

"Since your mother is determined not to have the baby today," I said, "and probably not until we are back in America, I'm going to make you some paper airplanes instead."

All gathered around to see how this might be achieved. I got a sheet of paper and folded it in a certain manner which I cannot explain, and then discovered that I was using a sheet from the manuscript of a book I was writing. So we got another sheet, and started again.

I folded the paper once and then made another fold. The kind of paper airplane I was making was not the dart kind that almost everybody knows how to make. It was the kind with wings, a fuselage, and a tail which every schoolboy in England learns to make before he can properly be passed out of the first grade. It is part of the democratic process of that country, no doubt, that the Prime Minister has made the same kind of paper airplanes in his proper resistance to learning as the man who removes the garbage from Number 10 Downing Street. These are not easy airplanes to make, calling for half a dozen or more careful folds of the paper, each to be done in its proper sequence. I started out confidently, but after two folds I was lost.

I tried again, and wound up with a paper boat.

I tried once more, carefully peering into the recesses of my memory to recall the right way to fold the paper. No good. I got a paper hat.

What had happened? Why couldn't I remember how to make the paper airplanes? I had made thousands of them.

I put all the forces of memory and reason to the problem and failed miserably. The children were beginning to feel embarrassed for me, and Patricia, out of sympathy, was prepared to argue that the paper hat I made was really an airplane if you just looked at it in the right way.

I quelled that kind of nonsense with a ferocious look and started again.

Somewhere, I knew, the knowledge of how to make that

paper airplane lay within me. I had had it once. It could not have gone. It was somewhere around, but I could not find it. Where was it?

I decided to try a new approach. In all my previous efforts I had tried to use my memory consciously. Now I would let my fingers and my hands have full control. I would let them do precisely what they wanted to do, having told them only that they were to make a paper airplane.

In a minute I had made one.

This was an astonishing discovery for me. I had always thought of memory as being a function of the brain. Was it possible that one also had memory in one's hands, fingers, feet, and in all the other parts of the body—all independent of the brain?

I tried once more making a paper airplane following conscious memory. I wound up with a boat again. Then I turned the job over to my hands, telling them to make me a paper airplane. They produced one in a matter of seconds.

"Hazel," I cried, "I've just made a shattering discovery! You know how you remember things . . . What's the matter?"

Hazel was sitting in a chair, her face white.

"I think I'm going to have the baby," she said.

"Cripes," I shouted, more or less to relieve my feelings, "just when I've found out how to make a paper airplane using the manual memory system. Hold on till I get the car started. Maria, Senhora having baby! Chama medico on the telephonaria or whatever you call it! Hurry!"

I dashed through the door into the rain with the children's cheers ringing in my ears and got the car started. Maria, meanwhile, called the doctor, who said he would meet us at the maternity home. Hazel had nothing packed because she was quite sure the baby wouldn't be coming for a while, and she finds it sad to pack for a baby which keeps delaying its arrival.

I didn't care if she hadn't anything packed.

I picked up a nightgown for her and a bed jacket and a packet of cigarettes and some matches and a deck of playing cards (she loves playing Patience), took her out into the rain to the car, and drove through the deluge to the maternity home.

There she was taken up to her room and I sat in a lobby downstairs, looking at the rain sloshing down on the geraniums outside the big French windows. It would be a girl, I knew. We had a boy, a girl, a boy, and a girl, and that was just too orderly. So it would be a girl and we'd call her Roxanne after the heroine of *Cyrano de Bergerac*.

All of a sudden it occurred to me, as I suppose it does to every father at these times, that my wife might die. I was overwhelmed at the thought and started up the stairs toward her, meeting the doctor who was coming down.

"Where are you going?" he asked.

"I'm going to tell my wife not to die," I said like an idiot.

"She will be all right," he answered with a smile.

I realized that I was making an ass of myself, so I went back to the lobby and watched the rain sloshing on the geraniums and felt oddly lonely, as if the whole world had been denuded of its population and I was left standing there, the solitary man on earth in the ringing emptiness of the world.

Finally the doctor came down and said I could go up and see her. She was lying in a bed in a huge room and looking very pleased with herself, and I felt mildly annoyed.

"The doctor says the baby won't come for some hours," she said. "Not until after dinner, at least. You'd better go home to the children. They'll be waiting."

But I've got a one-track mind when it comes to the important things.

"Listen," I said, "don't you go dying on us."

Hazel laughed. "I won't die," she said. "Now you'd better go back to the kids and have dinner with them and tell them I'm all right and the baby won't be coming for some time."

I didn't want to leave her but I thought about the kids. They'd be standing like I was, the four of them, up against the French windows with the rain sloshing down outside and thinking themselves the only people left on a lonely earth. I went back and told them the baby hadn't come yet but their mother was fine, and we had to have dinner, and then they'd all go to bed.

Maria was especially solicitous of me during dinner. She asked whether I felt well and if I did not want to lie down. She said if I spoke to the doctor I could have a bed in the same room with my wife, as that was the custom in Portugal. I remembered what Toni the taxi driver had said about pregnancy being harder on husbands than on wives. Maria said it would be better for me if I rested at the hospital during the coming ordeal. She would take very good care of the children, so that my mind was easy and my strength not overtaxed.

When I returned to the hospital, the nurse asked me whether I would not stay for the night and seemed concerned that I should be doing so much driving at such a time. I felt somewhat heroic in refusing the offer of hospitalization and saying that I thought I would be able to bear up until the baby was born.

The baby was in no hurry.

Hazel and I played cribbage for a long time and several times the doctor came in to inquire whether anything was happening. But nothing was happening except that Hazel was beating me at cribbage, and so he gave her an injection. Then another. And then another.

This series resulted in my beginning to feel unwell. I suppose it was autosuggestion. The lay nurses kept coming in and looking at me, sitting in the chair, smoking a pipe, as if they expected me to fade at any moment.

"Surely," I said to myself, "there may be something in the ancient belief that men should take to their beds when their wives are about to give birth. The natives of New Guinea do it to this day, and the natives of Ulster used to do it two thousand years ago. Of course my people come from Connaught, but maybe in Connaught they used to do the same thing."

Anyway, I began to feel unwell, and said I thought I'd go out for a bit. So I went out, had a cup of coffee, and came back feeling better, and played some more cribbage.

Hazel felt excellent all the time.

Then the doctor reappeared to introduce his daughter, a pretty dark-haired girl with a very pleasant personality.

She spoke English beautifully and told us that she had just returned from America where she had trained in a hospital in New Jersey as a registered nurse, passing the by-no-means minor medical examinations needed.

"You would like to go back to America?" we asked.

"Oh, yes," was the reply, "but it is very difficult. Three hospitals have offered me positions on their staff as a registered nurse. But the American consul here will not give me a visa."

"Why?"

She shrugged. There was no firm reason except a curious resistance on the part of the American consul.

We thought this nonsense and said so. Almost every hospital in the United States was crying out for trained nurses and could not get them. Here was a girl, dedicated to nursing, fully trained in America, her father was a doctor, specializing in gynecology, but she could not return to practice because of laws restricting the admission of immigrants.

The doctor plainly loved his daughter deeply and I fancy was not displeased that, for the time being at least, she would be staying here and using her training to help him. There was the nicest spirit of camaraderie between the two.

Finally Hazel's pains began in earnest. In America I would long ago have been banished to the men's labor room, there to smoke cigarettes, thumb through magazines, and anxiously eye every nurse who passed along the corridor, hoping for news. But here I was permitted to remain. I had not known before how intense labor pains are, or how the child struggled for admittance to the world. It is not a bad thing for a husband to know. He is, in my view, better employed knowing it than displayed as a tragicomic character in a waiting room.

The pains came closer and closer together, and the doctor told Hazel to take a deep breath and hold it when the pains came, as this would relieve them.

He gave no anesthetic. When the crisis was approaching, he wheeled her to the delivery room. I believe I would have been free to follow had I wished. I would have liked to have done so but remained behind only because I did not wish to distract the doctor or the nurse by my presence. And so I missed what is likely to be my only chance of seeing one of my children born, of seeing him leap triumphant into life after all his ordeal. I am still sorry about this.

I remained, then, in the adjoining room listening to the doctor encouraging Hazel. Finally, in the midst of his confident words of coaxing and encouragement, there came another sound—a sharp, angry squalling, vexed and impatient. I got up out of my chair and stood in the middle of the room, waiting. In a few seconds the doctor's daughter came in with our son in her arms.

He was a tough, red little bundle, with chubby buttocks and arms and back. There was a mass of dark hair on his head, and he was roaring with rage. The umbilical cord had been clamped off and severed but not yet tied. I was astonished at its toughness and the skill of its construction. I had never seen such a thing before. I followed the nurse into the heated room where she would tend the baby.

"Can I hold him?" I asked, and she gave him to me.

"Will you show me how you tie the cord?" I asked, and she showed me, explaining the process patiently and warning against the dangers to mother and child if the cord were improperly cut or improperly tied. I watched while the drops were put in his eyes, and while he was weighed. He weighed between nine and ten pounds, but the weighing was in kilograms and the scales not accurate. Then he was put into a tiny crib, standing on tall legs, so as to be bed high, and put beside his mother.

He promptly fell asleep. So did she.

I went home, and although it was three o'clock in the morning, Kevin was waiting in a chair by the fire for me.

"You have a brother," I said.

His eyes sparkled, as they always do when he is really pleased about something.

We sat down in opposite chairs to think of this new development.

"Gosh, Daddy," said Kevin at length, "did you have to go through all this waiting for me and Patricia and Christopher and Arabella?"

"Yes," I said.

He got up and came over and sat in my lap and looked into the fire. He was smiling slightly. We didn't speak.

It seemed to me then that the world would last a very long time and it was a good world.

15.

THE TOTAL COST OF THE BABY was one hundred and fifty dollars. Seven days at the maternity clinic, in a large private room with a beautiful balcony outside overlooking the Atlantic, was seventy dollars. The doctor's delivery fee was sixty dollars, and the rest was divided into small sums like six dollars for the pediatrician and five dollars to the nurses as gratuity. Hazel was obliged to remain in the clinic for a week, although she explained to the doctor she was accustomed in America to getting up on the second day and leaving the hospital by the third or the fourth at least.

He shook his head over all this advanced and rushed medical practice.

"I know," he said. "But it is better for you to stay in bed for several days. This early getting out of bed is not good, whatever they say in America. In later life your stomach muscles will sag if you get up too soon after the birth of your baby."

So Hazel stayed for a week, and I didn't mind at all. As a matter of fact this seemed the proper way to become a father. At home I had two servants looking after the children, preparing the meals, and doing the washing. And at the maternity clinic, instead of a little room smelling of disinfectants and with no view, there was a magnificent salon, with a breathtaking vista over the town and across the bay. I could stand on the balcony outside the room and see below the red-tiled roofs and little gardens and palm trees, the wonderfully carved chimneys, and beyond, the broad sweep of the mouth of the Tagus, with big ships coming in from the Atlantic and leaving for American or Mediterranean ports.

No house I have been in in my life, however luxurious, commanded the view offered in that ten-dollar-a-day room with its twelve-foot ceiling in which Hazel recuperated from the birth of her baby. And best of all the baby, whom we called Rory, was in the room with his mother. I could look at him at close quarters as he lay sleeping off the vast burst of rage with which he had entered the world. I was not, as with my four previous children, excluded from his presence for three days while he was displayed, at carefully regulated times, from behind the protection of a plate of glass.

The children came to see their mother in the hospital on the third day and crowded around the tiny crib peering at their new little brother. Christopher had a problem on his mind concerning Rory.

"I like him," he said. "But it's a pity he's Portuguese. When he grows up I won't be able to understand what he says."

The doctor, the nursing staff, Maria, Marco, Tomaso, and Celita were all very proud that the Senhora had had her baby in Portugal because the baby was thus Portuguese.

Each assured me that he would have the full rights of a citizen of the Portuguese republic and it was heartwarming to see how much pride they took in these rights. To be Portuguese—that was the finest thing in the world—just as we in America think it is finest to be American. I admired them for their patriotism.

Hazel, however, was somewhat concerned. We would have

to leave Portugal at some time, and on what kind of passport would little Rory travel? Just what was his nationality, anyway? We set out to clear up what was by no means a simple matter, for it appeared that Rory was an international figure.

We first had to register his birth, and this procedure demanded that we have with us two witnesses present during the time of delivery. The doctor was not available, nor was the nurse. Plainly they couldn't go with all the parents and register every child they delivered. The doctor was unconcerned.

"He is Portuguese," he said. "This paper work does not alter the fact. He is born here. Therefore your son is Portuguese. Any time he wishes he can come to his country—the most beautiful in the world—and claim the full rights of citizenship. I congratulate you." And that was as far as we got with the doctor.

I turned, as I did with many problems involving the regulations of the Portuguese government, to the lady at the real-estate office who had rented us the house. She consulted with her assistant and they agreed they would go with me to the Registo Civil to get the birth registered. To be sure they could not claim to have been present. But they were prepared to do their utmost on our behalf, and, as matters turned out, all went well.

But we were delayed at the Registo Civil by the fact that a bigamist had just been brought in for punishment. He was the veriest kitten of a man and attracted a huge crowd. He was tiny and shy, wearing a suit too big for him, and he looked like a child in his handcuffs. The women there eyed him with intense anger—a betrayer of their sex—and I had the feeling that given five minutes alone with him, they would tear him apart. But the men looked at him with a certain admiration. He had, in some small measure, evened the score for them. Confined, nay, condemned, by the sternest laws to taking only one wife at a time, here was a man who had taken two, as in the ancient pagan days, when a man with one wife was hardly a man at all.

Even the guards seemed proud of their prisoner's accomplishment and one of them gave him a cigarette—no small gift at all—and lit it for him. The official who attended to us explained the whole case in rapid French. The shy little man had succeeded in marrying two very pretty Portuguese girls, each in a separate village, and had maintained two households for several months before gossipy neighbors had led to the discovery of his bigamy.

The official's face beamed as he related these details.

"*C'est quelque chose magnifique,*" he said, and tugged his gray mustache.

I thought it magnificent myself. I have not the nerve for such an undertaking.

We finally got Rory registered, and he was issued with a *Cedula Pessoal*—the little black identity book of all Portuguese citizens—and a birth certificate. The *Cedula*, if he remained in Portugal, would record his whole progress as a citizen—the date he was of age to vote, his marriage, his divorce, when he entered the army (Portugal has compulsory military service for a period of seven years, I think), the date when his children were born, and the dates when he was sentenced to prison and released—if ever.

A whole plan of life, then, was laid out for him in this little black book.

The next step was to get him registered with the American consulate. This was easier. We just produced the birth certificate with Hazel's passport, and the registration was made. But

there was a hitch in getting the boy put on his mother's passport. This lay in the regulation stating that minor children's
pictures must be included on the passports of their parents
under American law. And the pictures must be of a particular
size and shot against a particular background. We were
stumped here, for I could think of no way of taking a child
of a few weeks to a photographer's studio to have a passport
picture shot. Snapshots, we were warned, would not do.

"How about his citizenship?" asked Hazel. "He will be
American, I presume?"

But this, it turned out, was not so. Since I am a citizen of
the republic of Ireland, Rory could claim American citizenship only if he resided for five years in the United States between the ages of fourteen and twenty-five.

And until then?

Until then he was Portuguese.

"He's Irish, too," I said. "Let's get him put on my passport. That ought to solve the problem temporarily."

Ireland does not maintain an embassy nor a consulate in
Lisbon. But she has a legation, on the second floor of a wonderful old creaky building, redolent with the atmosphere of
the decaying Georgian houses of Dublin. We climbed two
flights of creaking stairs and were met at the top by an ancient
and very courteous gentleman who showed us into a waiting
room. There was the very smell of Ireland in that room—a
smell compounded of horses and hawthorn, seaweed, damp
upholstery, strong tea, mud, aromatic tobacco, porter, furniture polish, the insides of upright pianos, soda bread, and even,
I fancied, a soupçon of incense. It was an Irish kind of place,
Victorian (for Irish furnishings and interior decoration have
remained frozen in the times of the plump Germanic queen)
and yet slightly raffish. There was a landscape on the wall

full of the sweeping motion of cloud and wind and tossing flowers which is the essence of Ireland, and some literature on a table dealing with salmon, pike, and trout fishing as well as where to book a room in Dublin during the week of the horse show. In the bookcase was a copy of Spinoza's *Ethics* cheek by jowl with a railroad guide.

"Is Ireland really like this?" asked Hazel.

"Yes," I said with pride. "It's a curious mixture of aspidistras and the most magnificent horses you've ever clapped eyes on. It's ancient, but is rendered youthful by age. The people enjoy the huge secret joke of life on earth, for they know they came from heaven and that's where they're going when they die. Ireland is probably the only place left in the Christian world where everybody really believes in eternal salvation. They have a saying there, 'God is good and the devil isn't bad—thank God.' "

The ancient gentleman returned, grave as a courtier, and yet with a smile in his eyes.

"May I have your passport," he said, "and the date of birth of your son? Himself will attend to you directly."

I gave him what was needed, and he returned in a few minutes with Rory's name on my passport and the necessary stamp affixed to it. No applications. No forms to fill out. No photographs. No instructions to call back later. No certificate attesting to the place and time of my own birth other than my passport.

"There's a fee of a dollar," said the man apologetically.

I had only the equivalent in Portuguese currency of a two-dollar bill.

"As one man to another," I said, "would it be wrong to ask you to keep the change and have a drink to my son?"

"I'll drink it in Irish whisky," said the old gentleman. And as we went through the door he added, "Rory O'Connor, the last king of Ireland." And I fancy he did a little jig.

So Rory turned out to be Irish Portuguese and a potential American, but it grieved Hazel slightly that he should not be automatically a citizen of her own country.

"Pay no mind to it," I said. "There hasn't been an Irishman born who wasn't, by reason of his birth, an American in spirit. All the pieces of paper in the world won't make a man a citizen of your country. Citizenship lies in his heart, and the Irish have American hearts."

16.

WITH THE BABY BORN AND THE car rebuilt, for that is what it amounted to, we were now in a position to travel around and see something of Portugal. Few lands have so much to offer in so small a space. We were there in the worst season, winter and early spring, when the rest of Europe is one big drab invitation to influenza.

But Portugal retains its brightness and splendor even during the wintertime. When other parts are wrapped in a burial shroud of weather, the azure crocus blooms in the Portuguese woods, acacia bursts with gold on the hillsides in December, and red lilies, bright as heated iron, thrust out of their dark-green foliage in December.

We were not long in our house at Malveira da Serra before we discovered that right behind us, farther up the mountain, were two of the most famous sights in Portugal. The first is called the Cork Monastery and the second, Sintra.

The Cork Monastery, a previous habitation of the Capuchin monks, is a delightful little place of cells, kitchen, chapels, dining rooms, corridors, and tiny gardens, all hewn out of the living rock. Because the rock was a bit cold and damp for sitting on, the good monks lined much of it with cork to offset rheumatism and arthritis. And then, perhaps to mortify themselves for this luxury, to remind themselves that all are travelers toward the grave, they embedded the skull of one of their fellows in the rock wall of the monastery garden where, brown and old, it grinned at them as they went about their duties.

This skull, in its particular setting, points to the high degree of artistic development among the Portuguese. It goggles down over an enchanting little garden, with the blue and delicate chalices of crocuses, each with its nugget of gold, sprouting stiffly up between the flagstones. There are gray stone seats around and splashes of geranium, red as blood, above them, so that loveliness and horror are placed exquisitely side by side. And is not that a picture of life?

We had visited the Cork Monastery, and Sintra, since they were so near, while Hazel was still pregnant. This was a mistake. The Capuchins must have been thin men of short stature. I could just about get around in the corridors they had cut in the rock to make their monastery. But Hazel got hopelessly jammed in the passageway between the kitchen and dining room and was only extracted by careful directions and adroit pushes from the taxi driver, Toni, and myself.

Despite this accident, no other place I saw in Portugal was as charming as this. The gardens lay like little pools of delight at every turning. Trees and shrubs grew over the monastery, since it was tunneled in the rock itself. The tiny chapels, with hardly room to stand, forced one to one's knees. They had an intimacy to them utterly lacking in large cathedrals, making you feel the personal presence of the Creator. But I would not have liked to have lived in the monastery. The cells were too much like sarcophagi, and in the moonlight the crocuses would be invisible, leaving only the skull smirking in the bare rock.

Sintra is farther up the mountain and it is a place of so many facets that it is hard to describe. To begin with, the mountain itself, as one goes higher, takes on a character all of its own. It is one of melancholy. The place seems even on sunny days always wet and dripping with sadness. White pockets of mist hang in the valleys, or are caught like wool in the tops of the trees. There are masses of ferns—themselves the saddest of growths—and tall trees, ivy hung. Camellias bloom here to perfection. Suddenly, climbing the road through this outdoor conservatory, you come to the village of Sintra. It is a lively enough little place, and if you stop at one of the restaurants, you are likely to be immediately informed where the toilets are—a most considerate gesture by the host to the traveler. (I believe it was the Duke of Windsor who, asked for a solid piece of advice on going from place to place with much time on the road, replied that one should never miss an opportunity to relieve oneself.)

Sintra is dominated by the Royal Palace, which sits in its own splendid square. It is a massive building in a bijou country and the kind of place you shouldn't try to see all in one day. This palace is a hodgepodge of architecture, for it has been built, added to, rebuilt, and added to again, so that a student of architecture could probably find in it a good example of every building school from the Moors to the Victorians.

I am no student of architecture.

True, I can recognize Gothic from Norman and I can tell fake Gothic from real Gothic, although more by feeling than by fact. But the architectural details expounded by the guide, in the most curious English I have ever listened to, made no impression on me.

We saw samples of tiling (*azulejos*) dating from the Moorish twelfth century to the mid-Victorian era and were shown a hole in the wall of a chapel through which the imprisoned king, Alfonso VI, heard Mass for almost ten years. We saw the Magpie Room—its ceiling is decorated with magpies and thereby hangs a tale. One of the Portuguese kings was found in this room kissing a serving girl. The news quickly spread through the palace and the king, asserting that his court consisted of nothing but chattering magpies, painted the ceiling with the birds in order to rebuke the courtiers.

How very Portuguese!

Hardly a king sat on an English throne, in more virile times, who did not kiss a serving girl and more than that, and never felt the slightest compunction in the matter.

There are other rooms, titled by their ceilings, in the Royal Palace at Sintra—the Swan Room, for instance, and the Mermaid Room. And in the center of the palace is a magnificent ceiling of wood, consisting of a series of geometrical designs that make you quite dizzy. To be sure this is decoration for the sake of decoration. But that in itself is an essential part of the Portuguese. Their art is not stern or strong. It is pretty and feminine, and how curious it is that some of the most hairy-chested travelers of the Age of Discovery—men who traveled so far afield that it was they who named the island of Formosa—should have been represented by a kind of wedding-cake decorative effect more fitted, in English terms, to a ladies' powder box.

Atop the mountain on which Sintra is perched is a huge outcropping of rock called Pena, and there is a palace upon this—certainly the biggest architectural joke ever built at enormous cost. It is a double joke—a joke in itself and a joke also in that it was built in earnest with no thought of humor.

The place is called the Palacio da Pena. Like the Royal Palace, it too is a mixture of every kind of architecture one can imagine, and all of it fake. A grim donjon keep in the center is rendered ridiculous by four pepper-pot towers on the corners with a large clock set in the four walls. There are pseudo Moorish arches cheek by jowl with pseudo flying buttresses, while minarets peek upon fake Norman ramparts.

All was done in earnest.

The place was built by Baron Eschwege, consort of the then Queen of Portugal, and the poor fellow thought he was taking the cream of every architectural period and producing a monument which would delight the world. And so it does in a manner which he had not foreseen.

The interior of the palace, however, is a work of peculiar genius. Hazel and I took a tour through the royal apartments and were filled with admiration at the undeviating bad taste of the furnishings. Never, in one tiny degree, did the decorators or the occupants blunder into good taste. To be consistently bad, exhibit even in the tiniest detail the most wretched eye for line, color, light and shadow, is surely a kind of genius of its own right.

The only other exhibit of this kind that I recall is the Albert Memorial in London—a sight so vulgar that it alone has been responsible for a mass of emigration by Englishmen to the dominions and colonies. Thousands of Londoners, to this day, hold it as one of the atrocities of the Luftwaffe that they never bombed the Albert Memorial.

We went, Hazel and I, through room after room of carved tables and carved chairs, artificiality piled on artificiality, stained glass in horrid hues making patches of odious colors on yellow upholstery and chocolate-brown chair legs—the legs carved with carving upon carving. There was not a straight line or a plain surface to be found anywhere. And yet in the center of this astonishing display we found a small chapel with pendent cords carved in alabaster before the altar, so beautifully done that as you watched them the carved stone cords seemed to be swinging slightly in a faint draft.

I nearly lost Hazel at the Palacio da Pena.

She came down a fake circular staircase under a pseudo portcullis, gathering momentum all the time, into the court-yard with a steep downward pitch toward a sham Norman battlement.

The drop over the other side was about a hundred feet and the battlement little more than waist high. As Hazel reached the courtyard she tripped on a cobble and dived toward the parapet.

I was aware that I might witness one of the most magnifi-cent swan dives ever executed but at the same time was about to lose my wife. I rushed forward and grabbed her while at the same time there was a resounding "crack" from some-where nearby.

My first thought was that Hazel had managed to set off some kind of alarm. But it seems that a toy cannon is kept loaded at the palace and when the sun reaches a certain angle its rays, focused through a glass on the touchhole, discharge the piece. Hazel had timed her near-swan dive for that exact moment, exhibiting a nice instinct for the dramatic.

There is one property of the Palacio da Pena which is un-excelled in all Portugal, and that is the view. From a hundred points on this ridiculous structure you can see across Lisbon and the Tagus River to the plains of the Alentejo and north-ward to Torres Vedras where Wellington established the English line which broke Napoleon's army in the Peninsular War. On a bright day, hills, valleys, river, tiny fields, and the jewel box of Lisbon itself—white, red, and green—are laid before you. You can pick out the little shreds of lacy water-falls on the mountain slopes and see the deep greens of ferns and treetops. Beyond is the rich brown of the plowed earth, and beyond that, the highway of the Atlantic which beckoned the Portuguese to fame in their greatest days.

It was from the eminence at Pena that the fleet of Vasco da Gama, returning from finding the sea route to India, was first sighted.

It was not hard, standing there, to recapture the scene as Da Gama's ships hove over the horizon and set their heads for the beloved Sea of Straw from which they had sailed.

I turned to Toni, the taxi driver, who was standing beside me. "Where can I pay my respects to Vasco da Gama?" I asked.

"He is buried in the Monastery of the Jerónimos in Lisbon," he replied.

"We must go there tomorrow," I said.

Toni hesitated a second. "I will charge you only half fare," he said. As a Portuguese he was proud of Vasco da Gama and did not wish to profit out of foreigners going to his tomb to pay their respects.

17.

IN THE GREAT DAYS OF PORTU-
gal, when that nation alone controlled the trade with the
Spice Islands of the East, crews signing up for the voyage to
Java first inspected the caravels to see whether they were
seaworthy.

The most important part of this inspection consisted of
going down into the hold and smelling the bilges. If the bilge
water was sweet, only green hands were likely to ship aboard.
But if the bilges smelt foul, the more experienced hands would
sign up. Foul bilges meant that the ship was tight: that she did
not leak much water. That was an essential property on
voyages which might occupy two or three years. Shipmasters
frequently poured foul water into the bilges of new vessels to
deceive the seamen. But an old hand could tell from the
general smell of the vessel whether she was soundly built or
whether her timbers would work in the Indian monsoon.

Sea lore is part of the character of Portugal, a part still
embedded in its people today. The coasts of Portugal are
dotted with fishing villages, and the Portuguese fish, like the
fishermen of western Ireland, in the Atlantic Ocean which
abuts directly upon their coast line. They build the most
beautiful fishing vessels I have seen, elegant in line, seaworthy,
with bows curved into a graceful crescent to take the ocean
rollers.

Seamen the Portuguese were, and it is as seamen that they

thought of themselves. Coral, sponges, dolphins, hawsers, seaweed, anchors, and spars—these are the motifs used most often in their carvings. The Torre de Belem, a fortress guarding the mouth of the Tagus and thus the doorway to Lisbon, is girdled around with a massive hawser, carved in stone, as if to lash it to the land, lest it be taken away by the great Atlantic ebb tide.

The greatest of the Portuguese seamen was, of course, Vasco da Gama. He was the man who launched Portugal into the world and brought that nation to the pinnacle of its fame. The Mosteiro dos Jerónimos is essentially the church of Vasco da Gama. It is a monument to him and all the riches he gave his country as a result of his pioneering. The Jerónimos then, lying in the outskirts of Lisbon, is the foremost shrine of Portugal, and it is excellently placed a little distance from the north bank of the Tagus, so the old seaman lies within hailing distance of the spot where he weighed anchor to set out into the unknown.

When we went to the Jerónimos, a guide immediately offered his services and we accepted. This proved a mistake. The man spoke English, to be sure, but with the high, flat intonation of a parrot so that it was extremely difficult to understand what he was saying. Yet he was most civil and anxious to help, and it was not his fault that though he had mastered the grammar and vocabulary he was handicapped with the intonation of a hysterical bird.

Before the present monastery was built, Henry the Navigator erected a little chapel on the site. It was called the chapel of Santa Maria de Belem (Holy Mary of Bethlehem). Its purpose was to provide a place where seamen, outward bound or returning home, could pray either for the protection of God or thank Him for their safe return. Da Gama knelt in prayer with his crew in this little chapel. And when he returned with the key to all the riches of the Indies in his pocket the then king, Don Manuel, the Fortunate, commissioned his greatest architect of the day, Diogo Boytac, to build the monastery.

A knowledge of architecture is not necessary to enjoy the Mosteiro dos Jerónimos. The whole concept is so lofty and so beautiful, the stone is so delicately carved, the stained-glass windows so magnificent in their color, that one is almost better off without architectural knowledge.

What Boytac achieved in this beautiful building was a picture in stone of the glories of the Indies. There is, for instance, a group of beautifully-carved pillars in the central part of the monastery. Each has a strange oriental cast to it. When you move off from these pillars and look back, you recognize them for what they are—a sculpture of a tropical forest, each pillar the trunk of a tree ending in palmlike carvings against the roof.

I have been in tropical forests many times. Once you get through the thick outer curtain of vines which proliferate wherever the sun will strike, you enter a roomy area of subdued light where branchless trunks of trees rise, in absolute stillness, upward toward the sun.

The effect is exactly like being in a cathedral.

And here in what might be called a cathedral, looking at the tree pillars of Boytac, the illusion of being in a forest was so strong that I half waited for the mocking pipe of a toucan or other tropical bird, or looked to find, in a sunny patch from a window, a jeweled constrictor snake warming its thick, heavy blood after hunting in the gloom.

Around the monastery are a number of chapels. My guide with the parrotlike voice named each of them and noted to whom they were dedicated or who lay buried before the altar. But I could not understand what he was saying, and had no means of asking him to be quiet, short of rudeness. One chapel was especially lovely, although he seemed to think little of it. The altar was either solid silver or silvered. It was all carved and lay in the dark, lit only by candles. The gentle light from the tapers dripped, soft as honey, over the silver; a sight so lovely that it will remain with me all my days.

But the guide was in a hurry and wanted to get us to the main tomb of the place. I thought this would be the tomb of Vasco da Gama, but I was mistaken. He ignored the tomb of the great navigator to bring us to that of Luiz de Camoëns (English spelling) the greatest poet of Portugal, and the hero and literary saint of the Portuguese people.

Camoëns was a distant relative of Da Gama, born in the year the sailor died—1524. He was a fiery young man of poor but gentle family, and a gifted poet. He lived the kind of life that the world at one time required of poets—a life of poverty and hazard, relying as often upon his sword as his pen for his fortune, but ever leaning toward the pen.

Banished from court for wounding an official in a brawl, he set sail for India as a common soldier, and when he decided to return was so poor that he remained for some years at Mozambique, unable to raise passage money for the remainder of the voyage. He was finally befriended and returned to Portugal. There he published, with the permission of the king, his epic poem *Os Lusíadas* (The Portuguese) commemorating the voyage of Da Gama, recounting the past glories of Portugal and looking toward the splendors of the future.

The poem is by every standard an epic and a monument of Western literature. It is scarcely known outside the Portuguese-speaking world, and I could not find, in any of the excellent bookstores in Lisbon, a single translation in English. But the city itself is pasted with cantos taken from *Os Lusíadas*. You may find half sheets, quoting a few lines of Camoëns, on many public buildings in Lisbon. It is as if in America we were so enamored of Whitman that we put extracts of his *Leaves of Grass* on posters and pasted them around New York, to lift us up during the course of the plodding day.

Camoëns' death was in keeping with his life. He succumbed to the plague shortly after returning to Portugal following seventeen years of enforced exile, and was buried in a common grave with other plague victims. The priest who performed the burial rites regretted that so great a genius had not even a sheet to cover his corpse. In 1884 Camoëns' presumed remains were exhumed and laid in their present sarcophagus, becoming by far the greatest shrine of the Portuguese nation.

There is a certain irony in this, at least for the outsider. Across the aisle from the tomb of Camoëns is the tomb of Da Gama. The crowds gather around the tomb of the poet. It is here that the little children are led by their whispering and reverent parents. Da Gama lies almost unheeded, solitary and apart. So, of course, he was in life—a doer rather than a singer of great deeds.

If it were possible to psychoanalyze a nation it might be said of Portugal that it suffers from a Camoëns' complex. The genius of this poet, and the bitter waste of his life, seem deeply to have afflicted the upper-class Portuguese, so that their attitude is one of melancholy. Their songs are sad and their clothing is habitually dark. Their attitude, even in the gayest moments, has an underlying tinge of mourning, which finds expression in the national music—the *fado*. The fado is literally a song of faith, but is misnamed, for both in its words and music, it is a song of despair. The melody has a sickroom talent, as Fielding said so rightly of the music of Chopin, and to attend a fado session in one of the many Lisbon taverns where these take place, is to indulge in a morass of musical despair or, at least, depression.

This is not to say there is no beauty in this music. There is a great deal of it. But the effect on the spirit is wearying. I never learned sufficient Portuguese to be able to translate, while it was sung, the words of a fado. But here is a typical verse:

> Two small candles are my eyes,
> Lighting my face with sadness.
> My face is marked with anguish
> Of parting and sorrow.

So sings the *fadista* to her melancholy and adoring audience. But not the happy peasant of Portugal. His are the songs of the earth and of the crops that the earth produces. He is merry where the upper classes are melancholy. One of his oldest songs, the inseparable companion of the second bottle of wine, goes something like this:

> I know a wine, dear God, a wine,
> A wine which I love deeply.
> And only death, dear God, only death
> Will end my drinking of it.
>
> When I die, let it be in a wine vault
> With a cup of wine in my hand.
> And may a barrel, dear God, a barrel
> Provide me with a coffin.

When I first came across this excellent drinking song I called Maria and recited a verse of it to her and asked if she knew it.

She blushed with pleasure and embarrassment but refused to sing it for me.

"Ah, Senhor Leonardo," she said, "when my father was drinking wine he loved to sing that song. The men would sing with him and my mother would scold him. But he sang it all the same and went on drinking. It is *muito antiqua* [very old]."

And so it is, for this particular song, like so much that is Portuguese, may be traced back to the Middle Ages. (In my own drinking days I recall a song of similar sentiment which may be derived from this ancient ditty. It went:

> When I die, don't bury me at all,
> Just pickle my bones in alcohol.)

The Portuguese, whose great men of the sea include Bartholomew Diaz de Novaes, who rounded the Cape of Good Hope in 1488, and Diogo Cão, who reached the mouth of the Congo River in 1482, and Pedro Alvares Cabral, who the Portuguese claim discovered Brazil in 1500, are niggardly in their attitude to the great navigators of other nations.

Ferdinand Magellan, although Portuguese and born in the remote district of Tras os Montes (Behind the Mountains), is scarcely honored though he was the first to circumnavigate the world. (He was, it will be recalled, killed in a silly war in the Philippines on his return, but had reached waters where the way home was well known.) Magellan sailed under the flag of Spain, having been refused employment, despite brilliant past services, by the sovereign of Portugal. The Portuguese have a historic dislike of the Spanish, and so Magellan is without public honor.

So also is Christopher Columbus.

To be sure he was Genoese, not Portuguese, and he also sailed under the Spanish flag (with a Galway Irishman as boatswain according to the Irish). Yet it was from Portugal's Tagus River that he set out to discover the New World. I could find no marker on the spot from which he set sail, and although New York boasts a Columbus Circle, Lisbon lacks even a statue to the great discoverer. This is surely carrying a provincial animosity too far.

Outside Lisbon there is a little fishing village called Cascais. And it is a Portuguese legend that two fishermen from that village were the first to discover the North American continent. They told their story to Columbus when he was in the Azores, producing a logbook to prove their tale, and it was through them, according to the Portuguese story, that Columbus first got on the track of the land across the ocean which he mistook for the Indies.

Maybe this is true. Fishermen from Cascais were the first to bring news to the Portuguese sovereign, then exiled in Brazil, of the defeat of the armies of Napoleon and the liberation of Portugal from the French. They set out on their own hook, without credentials, and beat the official emissaries with the good news by several weeks. I do not know what they got for their pains, and when I tried to check the story, several assured me of its truth, but none could remember the names of these patriotic fishermen.

When we had finished our tour of the Mosteira dos Jerónimos we went to the Torre de Belem, a little toy of a fortress built on the Tagus to guard Lisbon. The fortress is a child's thing—delightfully carved, every pillar in it decorated—fashioned as if a boy had decided to build a fort out of a tiered birthday cake. Nothing in all Portugal is as Portuguese as this. There are perhaps a score of small pillars forming a square balustrade on the lower level of the fort and each one of them is carved with a different design. The fort was ordered as a military installation, but obviously the artists got the upper hand of the military planners, for there are so many little carved pillars and copings and pepper-pot towers that under any kind of a bombardment the defenders would soon have been massacred by flying chips of stone.

That is what is so Portuguese about it. Things designed with the sternest of purpose evolve into charming toys, as if the Portuguese could not tolerate sternness for any length of time.

And yet the fortress towns that face the Spanish frontier—Elvas is a classic example—are as stern and forbidding as the castles of the Welsh Marshes.

All of Portugal's invaders came overland.

Therein, without a doubt, lies the reason why the fortresses by the sea are like toys and the fortresses of the interior as grim as a hangman's noose.

18.

THE NATURAL COURTESY AND manners of the Portuguese disappear when they get behind the wheel of an automobile.

The same, of course, is true in America, but not to the same extent. The American, even in his car, is likely to retain some regard for the rights of his fellow men, and does not, when driving, look upon pedestrians as his natural quarry.

But the Portuguese, given a car, has little or no consideration for the pedestrian. The only time I was really angry in Portugal was when a woman, driving a car quite slowly up to a stop light almost crushed Hazel against a wall in her efforts to slip up beside the car ahead.

I was so furious that I offered to take the lady from behind the wheel and spank her soundly. The offer, being made in English, fell on deaf ears, and the doors of the car were, perhaps fortunately, locked.

In olden times the mounted man regarded himself as superior to the man on foot. He would ride him down as a peasant or jostle him out of the way as if he were but one of a flock of sheep. This way of thinking remains today in Portugal (in Spain and France and Italy also) among car drivers, and governs their relations with pedestrians. Thus when you are walking in Portugal, particularly outside Lisbon where the police are on your side, you are in constant peril of mayhem from automobiles. Drivers vie with each other upon the road, like gladiators in an arena, scorning any kind of cooperation such as hand signals. They pull out from the curb with scarcely a glance to the rear, or cross in front of you as if you were not there. It early became plain to me that to do any kind of driving in Portugal I had to learn to drive all over again in this callous and careless continental fashion.

My initiation into the technique of driving in Portugal took place one rainy January day on a four-lane highway outside of Lisbon—the Estrada Marginal. The highway follows the coast out to Estoril, and I was bowling along handily in Rover, perhaps clocking a modest ninety kilometers (fifty-four miles) an hour, when I encountered, ahead, a Citroën DS-19 proceeding quite slowly. I pulled into lane number two to pass the Citroën and immediately set off a race. The Citroën speeded up. A Mercedes which had been tagging along behind me pulled into lane number three and a Volkswagen which had been behind the Mercedes zoomed into lane four.

Four abreast then, and with the Mercedes and the Volkswagen on the wrong side of the road, we swept forward in the blinding January rain in obedience to the first principle of continental driving which is: "Never let anyone pass you without a fight."

A sweeping hairpin bend loomed out of the gloom. I floored the accelerator and managed to stir Rover's ambition to the extent of 110 kilometers an hour. At the same time I sounded my horn—more or less to relieve my nerves. The Citroën zoomed up to 110 also, shouting, as it were, *"Vive la France! A bas l'Allemagne!"* L'Allemagne, represented by the Mercedes and the Volkswagen, followed suit. Still four abreast, we entered the hairpin, our horns giving out with a chord which would have brought a beam to the features of Johann Sebastian Bach.

At this point I lost my nerve and disqualified myself, temporarily, as a continental driver. I backed off on the accelerator, touched my brakes gingerly, and fell behind the Citroën. It was as well that I did, for a little Fiat 600 came steaming out of the rain and flung through the gap which I, coward that I was, had created in the previously solid front of France, Britain, and Germany. The Fiat 600 was also sounding its horn—a mite off A sharp, I fancy, though I was in no condition to give critical attention to the note.

I then pulled to the side of the road, set the handbrake, and after four or five shaky efforts managed to light a cigarette.

"It's a pity we spent all that money getting this car fixed," I said. "I don't think I'm going to do any more driving in Portugal—or anywhere in Europe, for that matter."

Hazel is of pioneer American stock. Her ancestors didn't just drive a covered wagon across the plains, the Rockies, and the Sierra. They raced theirs, damning the covered wagons ahead and those behind.

"If you quit now," she said, "we're through."

She unrolled the window and put her head out. "Animals," she roared, like Davy Crockett at the Alamo, so I knew that I had to drive like a European driver.

For weeks I drove in anxious anticipation of death, my right foot hopping alternately from accelerator to brake, and I found myself bullied all over the road. If I wished to pull away from the curb, no one would let me. If I wished to overtake a car ahead, the action was misinterpreted as a challenge to another race. If I put out my hand to signal a turn to the left, I was in danger of having it mutilated by a car which chose that very moment to zoom up from behind and pass on my left.

Finally, in desperation, I got myself into the right attitude of mind. Basically it is an attitude of being firm and confident. It is one that contradicts all United States driving experience because it insists that you let the other fellow get out of *your* way. You never get out of his, except in the final moment before impact. With this and some knowledge of the unofficial rules of the road most people can learn to drive in Portugal or elsewhere in Europe with a tolerable degree of safety—but only one half as safely as one drives, say, in midtown New York City.

Another one of the basic conditions of Portuguese driving is that, in practice at least, there is no such thing as the wrong side of the road.

The solid double line, familiar to Americans and marking a "no passing" zone, is largely unknown in Portugal. If you have the nerve, you can pass in the left-hand lane on a hairpin bend, and it is surprising how many Portuguese do this without meeting headlong an oncoming car, reducing both drivers to a few hundred pounds of butchered meat and several tons of automobile parts.

To ensure himself against such a misfortune the Portuguese passing on a corner on the wrong side blows his horn in a sustained and hair-raising blast. I was never present when there was an answering blast, and so witnessed no fatal accidents. But the accident rate is high all over the continent, and the matter is not helped by the fact that draft oxen hidden around a bend have no means of announcing their presence.

These draft oxen are common on country roads, particularly in the mountainous parts where donkeys are unable to haul the required loads. The oxen don't know their left foot from their right, and neither does their driver. It is an uncommonly unpleasant experience, on a twisting road, to round a bend and find the highway ahead completely occupied by slow-moving oxen with horns that appear twelve feet long. The only safety lies in anticipating such a disaster at all times, keeping your speed down, making sure that your brakes are in good condition, and being prepared to take to the hedge.

Driving in the country areas of Portugal, I soon learned to watch the shoulder of the road, calculating whether I could dodge onto it in an emergency. You must, in short, learn to regard the shoulder of the road as part of it. And this means driving more carefully on those roads (and there are many of them) which are lined on both sides by inhospitable stone walls.

Only men with strong nerve should do any night driving in Portugal. It is not that the roads are indifferently marked—they are excellently marked, excelling, in some respects, the marking which we are accustomed to find in the more advanced American states.

Rather, the danger lies in the country folk of Portugal, the dwellers in the tiny villages which dot the little republic. Portugal is a nation of such tiny villages and small towns. And the people who live in them use the roads as a nighttime drawing room. Lacking such household amusements as radio and television, without a cinema in many cases, they congregate after dark in the middle of the road, standing in groups on every corner, talking over their affairs until late at night.

Worse, they are invariably dressed in dark clothing. Worse yet, the streets of these hamlets and towns are not illuminated. And so you drive into a little village which you assume to have gone to sleep a long time ago, to find the whole population standing in the middle of the roads, and loath to move out of your way. If you are driving too fast, if the road is wet, or your brakes in poor condition, you can kill someone quite readily in these circumstances.

Portuguese drivers blink their lights furiously and rely on this instead of a horn obbligato to get them through these situations without damage. For myself I found it advisable to slow to a crawl on the outskirts of the village, and go through at the same pace. The night hazard within these villages is matched by another on their outskirts—this in the form of dark bicycle riders on dark bicycles. These wing along silently in the middle of the road, three or four abreast, leaping out of the dark into your headlights very unwilling to give way. Again the answer is to slow down and go gently past, though once more the native driver just blows his horn, flashes his lights, and keeps going.

Lisbon is probably one of the most nerve-racking cities in the world to drive around at nighttime. It has adopted the laws of Paris and of London, prohibiting the nighttime sounding of horns within the city limits and demanding that only parking lights be used while driving in the city after dark.

The first prohibition puts the heaviest strain on the nerves of the Portuguese motorist, depriving him of his chief weapon for getting his own way, or at least relieving his feelings.

He is reduced to flashing his headlights on and off, and most continental cars have a flicker switch whereby this is done automatically. The result is that one drives around with flashing fireflies on every hand—behind, ahead, to the right, and left. This is even more distracting than automobile horns. And Lisbon, unlike Paris and London, is an extremely poorly-lit city. There are overhead lamp standards, to be sure, but not enough of them. And there is little of that auxiliary lighting from shopwindows which one finds in American cities.

After-dark driving in Lisbon, then, is like groping around surrounded by myriad fireflies—all of them capable of killing —one's own way illuminated by a flickering candle. I found the best way to get about Lisbon after dark is to memorize the trolley-car routes and then tag along behind one headed in your direction.

I must confess myself completely baffled as to the Portuguese laws governing left-hand turns. The best I could discover was that you must not make a left-hand turn when the light is green, and you must not make a left-hand turn when the light is red. This leaves only the yellow interval, and I am not sure that it is lawful to make a left-hand turn even then.

However, since one must turn to the left occasionally, I found the best method is just to watch for your chance and then take it boldly. You may be admonished by a whistle from a policeman, but the Portuguese police are extremely polite. I got only one traffic ticket in Portugal, and that wasn't really a traffic ticket. I had parked my car unknowingly in a no-parking zone while shopping. When I came out it was to find a gaitered policeman, with gun and bandolier, towering over the car and looking very tough.

"*Boa noite,*" I said cheerfully, peering over a sack of American goodies—corn flakes at sixty cents for a small packet, frankfurters at a dollar a can, baked beans at seventy-five cents a can, and so on.

"*Boa noite,*" said the policeman, and politely opened the door of the car while I put the groceries inside.

Then he stood erect and saluted, leaving me without any return gesture adequate to the occasion. He took a pad out of a pocket with that deliberate and slightly menacing air common to policemen all over the world.

He tore a leaf off his pad and gave it to me. It was in English and said:

"You have parked your car in a bad place.

"It is illegal to park your car in the place where you have put it.

"Please do not do this again.

"Happy vacation. And come again."

I was deeply touched. I've never had a more pleasant traffic ticket in all my life. And I never again parked my car in an illegal zone.

Twenty years ago, I'm told, Portuguese roads were so bad that car passengers were wearied by as little as a fifty-mile drive into the country. There was so much bumping and jolting over potholes and gulleys that it was a common practice to reverse the car up some roads, just to give the passengers a chance to rest their weary neck muscles.

All that is now changed.

All over the land there are excellent tarmac roads clearly marked on road maps.

Second-class roads are likely to be the old stone macadam kind, and we never got into any trouble, even on these. Third-class roads I never travel on, even in the United States, so I cannot report on their condition in Europe.

But it is a mistake to bring an American-size automobile to Portugal for several reasons. Indeed, as we had already discovered, it is a mistake to bring any kind of automobile to Europe because of the really rough handling they get while being loaded aboard the ship in New York—and probably in other United States ports.

For European driving, American cars are much too big. They are magnificent machines for the job for which they were built—that is, crossing the continent on fast, straight roads, or driving four or five hundred miles in a day on a business or pleasure trip. In this field there is nothing to touch them.

But European roads, excellently surfaced as they may be, are not like American roads. They follow ancient highways, winding around innumerable corners, and climbing up and down hills. In this country we cut a road through a hill. In Europe the road goes over the hill. This is a heavy strain on our kind of suspension, and with the geared steering of the Detroit automobile, a man can wear his arms out in half a day's driving anywhere in Europe just spinning his steering wheel to take corners.

Then, again, there is the question of the price and quality of gasoline.

Most American cars will hardly run on the gasoline generally available in Europe. The ignition has to be heavily adjusted if the engine is not going to sound as if it is about to fly apart at any minute.

Then the price of gasoline is enormously high. We paid seventy cents a gallon in Portugal and one dollar and ten cents a gallon in France—and French gasoline (even high test) is first cousin to kerosene. This low-quality gasoline gives very poor mileage. In the United States Rover will comfortably do twenty miles to the gallon. In Portugal that figure fell to sixteen miles. In France it dropped to about twelve, so that for us, with an English car, automobile travel in France cost around ten cents a mile. If we'd been driving a Buick or a Pontiac we might well have been paying fifteen or twenty cents a mile for French travel.

Once we all went to visit the town of Elvas, a fascinating medieval fortress city completely surrounded by a wall, which guards a portion of the eastern frontier of Portugal. The wall

that surrounds Elvas is about fifty feet thick—such walls on
their interiors housed part of the population in medieval times.

The passage through the walls that surround Elvas is not
just a straight tunnel. It penetrates the wall for perhaps fifteen
feet, turns at a right angle to travel within the length of the
wall, and then turns at another right angle to give admittance
to the city-fortress. The central portion could be blocked off
in time of siege by dropping heavy gates. If a troup of invaders got that far, the gates were dropped in front and behind them, and they were liquidated at leisure by pouring
hot oil or hot lead or anything hot available on them from
above.

Ahead of us, on the road as we approached Elvas, was a
large and beautiful Cadillac. The driver entered the tunnel
into the wall and was confronted with the job of making a
right-angle turn with solid and seven-hundred-year-old
masonry on either side. What he should have done was back
out and explore Elvas on foot. But the problem presented a
challenge, and he was not going to be defeated by it.

He started backing and filling, moving forward a few
inches and back a few inches, and denouncing this ridiculous
tunnel in this ridiculous wall which, excellent as it may have
been at repelling the arms of Leon, was a confounded nuisance
when it came to driving a Cadillac.

This performance continued for perhaps forty minutes. It
attracted a huge crowd, ourselves among it. There were men,
women, and children, peasants and policeman, grandson and
grandsire, donkeys and goats and dogs and chickens, all
watching, and all (and I include the chicken) with a smile
upon their faces. After forty minutes, with a cheer from the
crowd, the Cadillac driver finally managed to negotiate the
first right-angle bend. His car was now in the center of the

walls of Elvas, with a right-angle bend ahead and a right-angle bend behind.

"Let us go around the other side and find an alternative road into the city," I said to Hazel. "This genius is going to be here all day."

But Hazel was for entering the town on foot, and this we did, and a jewel of a place it proved to be. Elvas is famous for its dried plums. Packed in wooden boxes, they gleam like dark jade. They are sun-dried, but sun-dried in some magical way, for far from being tough and juiceless, they are soft and sweet and retain all the essence of the original plum. You can buy dried figs and dried cherries (I think) in Elvas, too, and all these dried fruits, immediately reminiscent of childhood and Christmas, are to be had for a few cents a box. We were enchanted with Elvas. Fortified, it is built on the crown of a hill, the streets so narrow that they always seem crowded, for there is hardly enough room for the population, let alone the hundreds of Portuguese who stream in and out each day.

We passed saddlers' shops where splendid saddles are made to order and sandals and belts and all kinds of leather goods are to be had for very little. The sun was shining brightly and the streets, being narrow, were filled with lovely dark shadows, beckoning and adventurous. There was about the town the smell of leather and of animals, of dried plums and baked bread, of wool shawls and shavings of wood—indeed all the smells that belong to the Middle Ages and which we, living in modern cities of the industrial era, know little of. To as much as sniff the air of Elvas is to be taken into another and more leisurely world—to savor at first hand both the industry and the wholesome produce of men.

We found an open-air market with dark-faced men and women, cheerful as gnomes, presiding over mounds of vege-

tables and fruits, mostly the little red-gold tangerines which
are properly called Portugals. We bought a sack of these
Portugals from a woman draped, as are most of the Portuguese country folk, whatever the temperature, in a heavy
black woolen shawl.

Among the stalls were mounds of gaudy blankets and
pieces of pottery and wonderful baskets in every kind of
shape, and various wooden implements. I regretted that we
had not brought the car with us, for I would love to have
loaded up with the simple and enchanting treasure of the
market place of Elvas.

We spent perhaps an hour in this town and then returned
to where we had left Rover.

The crowd was still about—grandson and grandsire,
shawled women and brown children, donkeys, goats, and
smiling hens.

And the pink Cadillac was still in the middle of the wall.

"What do you think they will do with it?" asked Kevin.

"I don't know about now," I said, "but seven hundred
years ago they would have poured boiling oil on it by the
bucketful."

For all I know the Cadillac is still there, like a fragile pink
insect fossilized in gray rosin.

The Phoenician Village

19. EVER SINCE I HAD ARRIVED IN
Portugal I had been yearning to go to Nazaré. Nazaré is a
little fishing village about two thirds of the way up the
Atlantic coast line. But it is more than a fishing village. It is
a place solitary from all the world, populated by a people
who have their own dress and their own customs—as clannish
as the highlanders of Scotland two centuries ago. The boats
of the fishermen are different from those to be found elsewhere, and even the features of the people are different. All
this I had heard and all this whetted my appetite. I was tiring
a little of the luxury of our villa on the mountain outside of
Malveira da Serra, with its two and a half acres of garden and
its Japanese garden behind, with the little pool of goldfish
and a domestic staff of four.

I wanted to live for a while in a real fishing village and help
with the hauling in of the nets laden with gleaming fish.

"Let's go to Nazaré, see what it's like, and whether we can
find a house to rent there," I said.

"Swell," said Hazel, who would give the same reply if I
proposed residence in Lhasa, Tibet.

So we loaded everybody into the car, including Maria and
Marco, but not including Tully, the bulldog. This was quite
a feat, for Tully, as soon as the car door is open, plunges inside, and since he weights sixty pounds and is full of determination, it takes two strong men to hurl him out again.

We had bought for Rory a little portable cot. It was a kind
of canvas cradle with two handles on it like a shopping bag,
and he could be carried around with ease in this excellent
container. He proved a born traveler and lay in his cot on the
seat between Hazel and me making little singing noises to
himself. In the back were Maria, Marco, Kevin, Patricia,
Christopher, and Arabella.

This was quite a load for a car the size of Rover, but no
load at all really, when compared with what is expected of
most cars in Portugal. I commonly passed Volkswagens with
half-a-dozen adults jammed in their interiors, the driver thrust
almost halfway out the front door, with the steering wheel
and other controls off to his right.

There is a fine tarmac road from Lisbon up to Oporto in
the north, though it winds about on itself so that if you are
in a hurry you are likely to develop indigestion from sheer
frustration.

We were not in a hurry, and enjoyed the trip immensely.

We dawdled up cunning little hills and down their sides,
finding a change of view with every hundred yards. At one
point there would be a patchwork of tiny fields on a hill
opposite us, separated the one from the other by stone walls
which put me in mind of the west of Ireland.

At another we would round a corner to enter a pine wood,
cool and fragrant with furze bushes displaying golden flowers
in their depths. Or we would catch, in a cleft of a valley, a
glimpse of the Atlantic like an aquamarine in a wedge of gold.
All along the road, at intervals of perhaps two miles, were
road workers, though I came to think of them as road
gardeners. Theirs was the job of keeping the road edges
trimmed and tidy and they edged the grass on the roadsides

as neatly as a lawn. Whenever they see a car approaching, these gardeners of the highways stop and remove their hats, giving a most graceful bow. All the children and people waved to us as we drove past their villages, and we waved back to them. Marco had on the fine jacket with the fur collar which we had bought him through our grocery money, and seemed splendid indeed. I have no doubt that he was mistaken for the important owner of the car and I but the chauffeur, but it did not matter in the least. We had a marvelous drive through a fairy landscape, noting how even in winter the flowers bloom in Portugal.

At one part we came to a field in which white blooms lay thick as lamb's wool.

"What kind of flowers are those?" I wondered, and got out to investigate. They were narcissus—wild narcissus, acres of them spread lavishly through the verdure. I picked a bouquet and brought them back to Hazel. Farther on, by the side of the road, were iris—azure iris, cool and tall, beautiful as Dante's Beatrice.

Delight then lay on every hand. We pointed out the sights to each other and sang snatches of song and laughed and asked Maria and Marco all kinds of questions which they were quite unable to answer. The country through which we were driving was as new to them as it was to us.

Finally we reached the little city of Caldas da Rainha, which means the Queen's Bath. In the center of the city is a statue of Queen Leonora, the founder. The good lady, traveling one day in her carriage, had noticed some of the peasants bathing in foul-smelling mud on the side of the road. She inquired what was the purpose of this lunacy and was told that the mud was beneficial in curing many kinds of aches. So she established a royal bath in the area where she could wallow in the mud like the peasants. Thus the city came into being.

At Caldas da Rainha we stopped for lunch. The meal was distinguished only by the fact that Marco ate two luncheons from soup to sweets and seemed ready to eat a third, but Maria prevented him. A Portuguese lunch is the major meal of the day and consists of soup and salad, a fish course, a meat course, and a sweet course followed by cheese. I could never get through the menu although I have a good capacity. But the people of Portugal, children included, delight in their food and readily encompass these meals.

Portuguese cheese, incidentally, of whatever variety, is among the best in the world. There is a kind called Queijo da Serra (Mountain cheese) which is soft and creamy and has a most satisfying taste, somewhere between sharp and full. It is made, I believe, from goat's milk and can scarcely be had outside of Portugal, for it will not travel and preserve its goodness at the same time.

When all were full we went on to Nazaré, leaving the main highway to head toward the Atlantic shortly after quitting Caldas da Rainha. Nazaré has a quality of the sea that leaps upon you as the ocean itself does when, surrounded by land, you top a hill and find it astonishingly before you.

A series of sand dunes and minor hills hide this village of the sea from the main road and from the rest of Portugal. You turn down a little lane past a kind of lagoon, shallow and sandy. Every boy should have one to swim and row upon. And when it looks as though you are about to drive into the Atlantic, you turn right.

And there is Nazaré—Nazaré of the ocean; Nazaré of the

strange ships, Nazaré of the ancient world, and Nazaré of the tempests.

It is a white town, strangely oriental, the houses jammed one upon the other with tiny windows cut in their thick walls. The roofs are of red tile, the streets narrow, uphill, and cobbled. Doorways are like archways and you are in Nazaré for but a moment when you realize that the village itself is but a bedroom. No life exists there during the day. There are no hawkers in the street, no people about their marketing, no children chasing homemade balls around the steep gutters.

All are down by the seashore, leaving the town deserted.

The people of Nazaré are sea people who must sleep sometime upon the land, and for this reason they have houses. But the whole of the day they spend upon the beach, among their strangely-prowed fishing craft whose huge bows sweep upward like Arab scimitars—giant knives made to slice the sea which is the eternal foe of the people of Nazaré.

And strange people they seem indeed. Their features are those of Arabs—quite different in bone formation from the rest of the people of Portugal. Plainly they are a foreign race, their nationality is Nazarene rather than Portuguese, and their domain is not the land but that wild ocean whose surf thunders in their ears day and night. Their women are dressed always in black—black perhaps for mourning for the husbands and brothers and sons and grandsons they have lost to the ocean against which they pit themselves without thought of surrender.

There never was in all the world a more unlikely site for a fishing village than that of Nazaré. The whole beach is open directly to the ocean—three thousand miles of its unchecked sweep and power. There is no shelter for boats, no shelter for houses. A headland runs out at one end of the town but it is the kind that seamen avoid—sheer, cruel cliffs with granite rocks at their base. It is as if these fishing people had deliberately selected for their age-old battle with the sea an arena of which it could never be said the ground favored them. The beach rises swiftly up from the ocean, and since no boats can ride in this open Atlantic roadstead, all are hauled up on the beach when not in use—ponderous craft heaved out of the ocean by man, woman, child, and ox power.

The women show their prosperity by the number of petticoats beneath their black dresses. A young girl will have a modest two or three. But when she has acquired some estate in the world, a dozen petticoats, each of a different color, hang from her waist to make the edges of her black skirt stand out a foot or more from her calves.

The men wear colors. Alone among the fishing folk of Portugal they are clad in hand-loomed shirts and trousers of bright plaid—green, brown, yellow, blue, and red worked into wonderful tartan designs. None of these designs are ever repeated, it is said. A pattern is worked out for one man, and that remains his while he lives.

There are many theories for this tartan dress of the fishermen of Nazaré. One is that, centuries ago, a shipload of Scots, returning from some far voyage, was wrecked off this coast, settled there, married Portuguese girls, and taught them to weave the old tartans of their clans. Some pretend that the light hair of some of the people of Nazaré shows a Scottish ancestry.

But there is an older and, I think, truer belief! The Nazaré fisher folk are the remnants of a settlement of Phoenicians who in their time sailed from their home in the eastern Mediterranean out through the Pillars of Hercules, some going south to Africa and some north to the remote islands of Britain and Ireland. Plainly such people, world traders on a scale which we have not yet come fully to realize, had their settlements on the coasts of Europe on their route north to get some the rare red gold of Ireland, the soft white tin of Cornwall, and the shiny black jet of Whitby in the North Sea.

And it is not straining matters too far to theorize that Nazaré was such a settlement and that the colored shirts and trousers of the fishermen of Nazaré are a remnant of the bright clothing which the Phoenicians wore—a remaining trace of the biblical cloak of many colors.

Indeed, some maintain that fishing folk around the world are all of the same race (intermixed with other bloods to be sure), but tracing ancestry back to the Phoenicians, and this accounts for the similarity in the tying of knots which exists in fishing settlements thousands of miles from each other.

There is yet another theory about the plaid clothing of the Nazaré fishermen, each pattern individual to the wearer. It says these plaids serve to identify drowned men, whose features have been destroyed in the ocean. This appealed to me as being likely, for the plaid of the father is different from that of the son, and the woman who wove it would know from a scrap of cloth the identity of the body to which it clung.

When we visited Nazaré, the day was fair and the wind but gentle. Yet the Atlantic still hurled its challenge at the people of this undaunted village. The tide was full in and the beach, as I have said, slopes steeply upward. The heavy Atlantic swells rose in glittering green walls as they approached this beach to a height of six feet and then flung themselves upon it with such force we could feel the ground shake beneath our feet.

And all along the back of the beach were the black-shawled women, some of them in their eighties, staring at the ocean with ancient hatred. Some carried, muffled in their shawls, babies of a few months. The infants slept to the thundering of the surf against which, as grown men, they would pit their lives.

We found a tourist agency in the town, staffed by a bright young man and his wife. Since they both spoke French, it was possible to carry on some kind of conversation with them about Nazaré. The headland, on the north side of the town, rises several hundred feet up, so steeply that it would be an hour's hard labor to climb to the summit.

There is a tiny cable railroad, then, to carry the people of Nazaré up to this headland. On the headland are other houses and a church, but more important still, a lookout post, where a man is stationed, night and day, watching for shoals of fish passing offshore.

At night these may be seen readily enough, I suppose, by the phosphorescence in the water. By day, the shoal reveals its presence with splashes and leaps of individual fish. When such a shoal is sighted, an alarm is sounded. And day or night, irrespective of the weather, the fishermen of Nazaré launch their boats and take out after the fish.

Sometimes boats are gone for several days, for the men will follow the shoal for miles and not return until they have a full load. The fish are presumably gutted and salted in barrels of brine to preserve them. And when the weather is mild, the womenfolk remain on the beach, day and night, waiting for the return of the men.

There are a great number of drownings, and when Maria heard of this, her comment was, "Stupid people. Why don't they leave and go somewhere where they can work on the land?" The practical Maria would never understand the significance of Nazaré.

We inquired about houses to rent and were told there was a furnished house to be had not far from the ocean. I was delighted and we set off immediately to find it, the lady from the tourist agency coming with us. Nothing would please me more than to live for a time among such people.

But when we got to the house we soon discovered that it was not for us. It was not actually a house which was for rent, but an apartment, and where the stairs reached the upper floor there was no banister to prevent a fall down the stair well. I could see Arabella tumbling down there several times a day.

There were three bedrooms, so tiny that they could just contain a bed. The mattresses were sacks, slit down the middle, and filled each day with fresh wood shavings. There was a charcoal pot for cooking and no bathroom or toilet which we could discover. A younger couple, without children and of an adventurous turn of mind, would do excellently here. The rent was only twenty dollars a month. But with my family of five children, it was impossible.

So I didn't sleep on a mattress stuffed with wood shavings, or pull an oar in a Nazaré boat, with the Atlantic wind and the Atlantic spray flinging about my shoulders, or learn the songs that the fishermen sing or qualify to wear the plaid shirt of a Nazaré fisherman. And I'm sorry about it.

20.

PORTUGAL IS A DICTATORSHIP, and it is the kind of dictatorship that poses an interesting question for those of democratic principles: Is it possible that in some circumstances a nation can benefit by surrendering its political liberty? Put in another way, and perhaps a more practical one, the question becomes: Is it better to be hungry and have freedom, or to be well fed and not have freedom?

Most of us cannot answer that question because most of us have never been faced with these alternatives. We are politically free, and our country is generally prosperous. Nor does it depend for its prosperity on the genius and devotion of one man and one man alone.

The situation is not so in Portugal. Before the advent to power of Dr. Antonio de Oliveira Salazar in the mid-1920's, the Portuguese economy was in a chaotic state. The escudo was worth about two and a half cents, taxes fell largely on those who could not afford to pay them, corruption was rife, exports were falling, imports were unrestricted, and the budget was never in balance.

Today Portugal's budget shows a surplus each year, there are free schools, tuberculosis has been all but exterminated, a network of excellent roads covers the countryside, and the Portuguese civil service is among the best and least corrupt in Europe. And this is the work of one person—Salazar.

Salazar, dictator of Portugal, is a remarkable man in many

ways. Outside his own country little is known of him, and in Portugal little is said about him. Most Americans think of him as being a professor of economics who rescued the Portuguese economy. He is not a professor of economics, but a professor of law, and provides a shining example of a lawyer at the very top of his profession—he makes laws, personally, for a whole nation. And most of them are wise laws.

Salazar is unique in Western history in that he is the only dictator who resigned—and was then invited back. Most others in recent years have come to sticky ends. He is unique, also, in that he is personally loved by everyone in Portugal. He has no wife, no mistress, drinks rarely, avoids parties and other entertainments. His one love is his country, and when you are in Lisbon late at night, your taxi driver will point out to you a lighted window in the presidential palace in the heart of town.

"That is Dr. Salazar's study," he will say. "He is working for us even now—so late at night."

Theoretically Portugal is a republic. The government is headed by a prime minister—Salazar—who appoints a varying number of cabinet ministers to advise him. There is a National Assembly of one hundred and twenty deputies. These are elected as a block and are required to meet for at least three months out of every year, to rubber stamp the various measures for which the prime minister requires their approval. Since all these members are necessarily of the prime minister's party, there is no such thing as an opposition. There is a lower chamber in the Portuguese congress, a corporative chamber consisting of members of the various trades and professions. They advise and nothing more.

What Salazar has done, then, is to take the outward form of a republic and mold it to the purposes of a dictator.

And he is very much in earnest about this. Public criticism of his government is taboo. But to give lip service to the name "republic" a few months before the holding of a general election, the opposition is, in theory, allowed to hold public meetings and solicit the support of voters. The last time the opposition tried, the members were all arrested, their offices rifled, and the leaders jailed "for the security of the republic."

There is nothing here, then, but a dictatorship. The press is firmly muzzled and when, on entering Portugal, I wished to bring a personal library of books, I had to assure the customs people there were no books with any political content in my collection.

The depressing part about all this from the point of view of the democratically minded is that the dictatorship works. You will travel a long way before you find a peasantry happier than the Portuguese country folk. They are not only happy but well fed and of independent character on matters other than political. Most own their own houses and their little fields, they have a good market in growing cities for their produce. Their children get a better education than was possible for them under the rule of the former king. The health service is better. They benefit directly and indirectly from the growing tourist trade in Portugal. And they don't seem to care a fig about politics.

And yet when you have been in Portugal a little while you begin to sense the presence of this dictatorship of which the common folk seem quite unconscious. You sense it whenever you go for a drive in the country. In the remotest parts, and in the most pastoral scenery, you will find soldiers armed with rifles patroling the sides of the road.

Why?

Basically, because a dictatorship must have force behind it

—brutal violent force if need be. And this seems to be true however benign the dictatorship.

My first brush with the regime was in the minor matter of getting my books into the country when I assured the officials there were no political volumes among them.

A second brush, again minor, came when my brother-in-law sent us some presents for the children's Christmas.

We received a card saying that a parcel had arrived for us, and went down to the post office in Cascais to collect it. But the parcel, having come from the United States, had to be collected at a particular branch of the post office in Lisbon. Off we went to Lisbon the next day and located this branch with some difficulty. There we found a small man at a counter in a large room. The room behind and about him was stacked high with parcels, suspicious parcels which had been sent from abroad and which he might issue to their owners only after the most thorough investigation. It seemed to me that these parcels, handed out as they were at the rate of perhaps one an hour and arriving in ten times that quantity, must soon engulf the little man, come crashing about him, and set in motion a second Lisbon earthquake.

It took us an hour of waiting to get to the little man and show him the card we had received. He checked it against his files and announced that we were to receive two shirts and four toys.

I said fine, that I could do with some shirts, but I was not to have them that easily.

First, the little man explained, I must go to the Ministry of Economics and there get a clearance for the two shirts and the four toys. Here I began to see how deeply a dictatorship enters into the private affairs of people. In a dictatorship, the

Ministry of Economics rules the people, not the people the
Ministry of Economics.

We set off for the Ministry of Economics and were shown
into a small waiting room. There I was informed that I must
fill out six separate forms concerning these two shirts and
four toys which had been sent us for a Christmas present.
These forms were all identical, and when I discovered this, I
asked whether I might not have some carbon paper so that in
filling out one I could fill out all.

No. Carbon paper was forbidden. The forms must be filled
out in my own handwriting. Presumably they went, one a
piece, to six different officials in six different departments of
the Ministry of Economics—and therein lies another part of
a dictatorship. You must reward supporters by building up a
massive civil service whose whole staff is dependent for their
employment on the continuance of the dictatorship.

I think the Ministry of Economics expected that I would go
away and fill out these forms and return them later.

But I sat right down there and then and filled out the forms
—they had to be filled out in Portuguese, of course, and I had
to be most careful not to misspell the Portuguese word for
shirt or toys or the whole thing would be illicit. When I had
performed this task I gave them to the officials.

He took them away and we were left waiting again.

Then the official returned and told me to follow him.

I was escorted to a large office in which a number of clerks
were seated at desks. One, dressed in imitation of an Oxford
graduate—that is tweed clothes, rather loose, a bright yellow
pullover, and a soft knitted tie—got to his feet.

"Senhor Wibberley?" he asked.

"Yes," I replied.

"You are indeed Senhor Wibberley?"

"Yes."

"Then here is your permit." And he gave me the permit of the Ministry of Economics of the Republic of Portugal to go to the post office of the republic of Portugal in the city of Lisbon and there collect the two shirts and four toys without fine, imprisonment, restraint, lien, tax or fee whatever.

I went and handed the form to the man who was about to be crushed under an avalanche of parcels.

"So soon" he said in surprise. He turned to the others around and explained that it was only that very day—nay, but a scant two hours before—that we had gone to the Ministry of Economics to obtain the permit which he now held in his hand. He was delighted and proud of the efficiency of his government and kept repeating *"muito rapido, muito rapido."* We had probably been given special service as visitors.

For his own part, however, he did not propose to be *muito rapido.* All very well for the Ministry of Economics to put on a spurt of zeal, but matters went far more sensibly in the post office. I should now return to our home and the parcel would be sent to us there.

There was nothing I could do to change that fiat.

Two months later—that is to say in February—we got the two shirts and the four toys sent to us as Christmas presents.

My third and final brush with the regime occurred, I fancy, as a result of this. While in Portugal I had written a few articles about the country and its people for the Los Angeles *Times.* One of these, a laudatory article, was sent back to Lisbon by some correspondent in America and reprinted in *Dairias e Noticias,* the leading morning newspaper of Lisbon.

I now wrote another article, not so laudatory, telling about the struggle to get hold of the two shirts and four toys. This, I have every reason to assume, was also sent back, though it was not reprinted in *Dairias e Noticias*, to my knowledge.

A little while later I had to go to the police station in Cascais to renew our visas. The Portuguese immigration authorities, operating through the police department, usually grants visitors a visa for sixty days, which can be renewed for a further sixty days, and so on. There is no trouble to it. You merely write out a form letter in Portuguese on a piece of paper, attaching a five-escudo stamp, and hand it to the police at the nearest station, and the visa is automatically granted.

However, when I now called on the police for an extension of our permit to stay, matters went rather differently. Before, I had stood with the official of the police in a large room crowded with other applicants, all gathered around his desk trying to get attended to. Now, however, he cleared the room and invited me to sit down.

"Where do you live in Portugal?" he asked.

"In Malveira da Serra," I replied, surprised, for he knew perfectly well where I lived.

"What do you do for a living, senhor?"

"I am a writer."

There was a shocked silence. If I had said I was a Communist, the effect could not have been more marked.

"What do you write?"

"Books."

And again there was a silence and a sense of my having said something incriminating.

"What kind of books, senhor?"

"Books," I replied, "of political satire." This was not the whole truth. I write other kinds of books also, but I was not of a mind to mention them at this time.

The police officer flushed. "You are writing a book now, senhor?"

"Yes."

"Was it necessary to come to Portugal to write this book?"

"Senhor," I replied, "I could not have written it anywhere else."

He picked up my passport suddenly and stamped it and scribbled his signature at the bottom.

"Twenty days," he said.

"I applied for two months," I expostulated.

"Twenty days. At the end of that time you may return and apply again."

I went with Hazel to a little café where we used to have afternoon tea—wonderful cakes and tarts with jam and tea and truly heavenly buttered toast. There I picked up a copy of the *Daily Telegraph* and an item on page one caught my eye.

It read as follows:

PORTUGUESE TRIAL

Lisbon—Tuesday. Ex-Captain Henrique Galvao, 62, was sentenced to a further 16 years' imprisonment and 20 years' suspension of civil rights by a Lisbon court tonight. He was convicted of writing subversive and defamatory propaganda against the Government while serving a previous sentence.

—(BUP)

I showed it to Hazel.

"You know," she said, "I'm still wondering about those two people who came to look over the house the other day, saying they wanted to buy it."

"What about them?" I asked.

"Well, they hardly looked at the house, but spent all the

time talking to you. They asked you what you did, and you said you were a writer, and then they asked you what kind of books you wrote and you said political satires."

"So?"

"Well, the man asked you whether you didn't think that was dangerous."

"So," I repeated.

"I'm thinking," said Hazel, "of poor Captain Henrique Galvao. He seemingly said something about the government that they didn't like and they threw him in jail. Then he criticized the government once again while in jail and he got sixteen further years just to make sure of him."

I thought, munching on the buttered toast, about the captain. He might have been jailed originally for cutting someone's throat for all I knew. But it seemed hard to give him a further sixteen years' sentence for having the temerity while in a jail, which he had supported out of his own tax money, to write something saying he didn't like the government. In a sense, it was his jail and his government.

"You know something," I said. "This buttered toast doesn't taste very good. Yesterday it tasted swell, but today it tastes awful."

"I've been thinking about Ireland," said Hazel. "It must be a crazy kind of country. I think we ought to go to Ireland."

"It'll be raining all the time."

"Wonderful," said Hazel.

"Dublin is a terribly dirty city," I said.

"It can't be if it rains all the time," said Hazel.

"When the sun does shine," I said, warming to the idea, "it's so beautiful that you look up to see if Peter left the door of heaven open by accident. The mountains in Ireland show blue

over the horizon and the children say they are the foreheads
of giants buried in the ground."

"Blue giants?" asked Hazel.

"Of course. Irish giants are the most interesting in the
world. When I was a boy I used to go to a little stream which
had been blessed by St. Brendan and catch trout in it with my
hands."

"Who's St. Brendan?" asked Hazel.

"The man who discovered America. He sailed there in a
stone horse trough around about A. D. 600 and then he came
back again."

"Why?"

"It wasn't time for America to be discovered," I replied.

I talked on a bit more. It was thirty years since I'd been in
Ireland, and I began to realize that thirty years was too long.
I wondered if the rainwater still ran in silver streams through
the lush grass of the meadows, right over the grass, that is, so
you had a river with a bottom of turf to play in. And I
wondered whether the mackerel still rushed in out of the
Atlantic in late summer, ocean-hungry, chasing the little silver
sprats up on the beaches in bushels. And I wondered whether
the furze bushes still grew six feet tall and the fuschia ten and
twelve feet. And whether that cliff I had fallen down, trying
to get at a tangled fishing line when I should have been at
Benediction, was still there.

We paid the bill and went home, and I called the kids
together.

"We're going to Ireland," I said.

"*Bom*," they roared. "*Muito bom*," and Christopher said
he'd take his good old hunting knife in case of Indians.

That's the way we decided to set out for another spot.

We were really sad at leaving Portugal, but it seemed that

this was the time to go. It wasn't altogether the visa business, though that was a factor.

There was a great shout of the Gaels coming to me from across the Portuguese mountains, and I knew that if I stayed any longer in Portugal I'd be finding all kinds of Irish things around, as in California I had come at every turn up against something Portuguese.

And so we packed our sixteen trunks which had now grown to twenty-one, shipped them off, and said good-bye to Maria and Tomaso and Marco and Celita.

It was a parting of tears. Everybody wept. Maria kept saying, *"Desculpe. Desculpe"* ("Forgive me. Forgive me"), in remorse for her misappropriation of funds to keep the love of Marco, and we assured her there was nothing to be forgiven. Still weeping and begging our forgiveness, she realized that the source of her love tokens was about to depart and managed to extract from Kevin fifteen escudos he had saved.

Big Celita couldn't say anything at all. She just cried, and I patted her on the back and told her not to cry because we could come again next year. Even Marco, the most aloof of all, was dewey-eyed, and Tomaso bobbed and bit his lip to keep back the tears and pressed two packets of his precious cigarettes on me.

And so, with a shout of "Viva, Portugal" we went roaring out of the driveway and down through the village, out over the mountains, and across Spain and France and England to Ireland.

And when we got there it was raining exactly as I said it would be, but that is another story altogether.

21.

Since our return to America, friends have asked me many questions about living in Portugal which are not covered by Leonard in this book— largely because men are not fully conscious of such matters.

There is the question of schooling, for instance. We considered putting the two elder children, Kevin and Patricia, in the village school in Malveira da Serra. But the instruction, of course, was entirely in Portuguese and we felt that it might just have bewildered them and made them feel lonely and foreign, so we decided against this. We did hear of an English-speaking private school in Estoril, for the sons and daughters of English exiles. But the fees were more than we could afford. They were a hundred and sixty dollars per pupil per term, and there was no way to get them to the school four miles away (this was before the resurrection of Rover).

In the end, I decided to give the children daily lessons myself. I have my teaching degree, had taught first, second, and third grade in California schools, and so was able to give them lessons in reading, writing, and arithmetic. Social studies they had ample opportunity to pursue themselves. They found out a great deal about life in a Portuguese village simply by playing with the children there. They had soon made friends with the little shopkeepers—the baker and the hardware merchant, the milkman and so forth. They got on very well with the Portuguese children, though for some weeks they could hardly say an intelligible word to each other. A favorite recreation of theirs was to find a boy who had a donkey and then go for donkey rides. Sometimes Maria took them down to the beach to bathe. At other times, I lured Leonard away from whatever he was doing to make them bows and arrows. He taught Kevin to fletch (feather) his own arrows and make some very good ones. The children spent hours climbing around through the forests and fields picking wild flowers with their Portuguese playmates.

The most fascinating household problem was laundry. The laundry tub was of marble, with an attached marble wash-board. Being used to an automatic washer, I pictured our clothes disintegrating through constant vigorous scrubbing. But at least I didn't have to do the scrubbing myself, which was handled by Celita and Maria. A white wash took three days by this hand method for a family our size, and a colored wash, two. There was always the problem of waiting for a sunny day to get clothes dried and I had to keep after Celita constantly to have clothes washed and ready so we could take advantage of sunshine. Her method was to wait until the sun was shining and then start to wash; a prodigal waste of sunshine.

I finally got Celita to do things my way by taking over the washing myself. She was horrified, and thereafter washed whenever there was laundry to be done, rather than let it accumulate into a monstrous load.

A white wash took a long time because the first day the clothes were soaped and then laid out on the lawn to bleach. While there, they were constantly dampened. The second day they received another thorough scrubbing with soap and water, and finally, on the third day, they were hung up to dry. The result was a much cleaner wash than I ever produced with my automatic washer—but, oh, the problem of clothing my family with undershirts spending several days being washed and but one on the back.

The communal laundry in the village always intrigued me. As a matter of fact I envied the lives of peasant women. They were really more independent than a lot of my friends in America because they lived so simply. Their homes were modest and easy to keep clean.

The Portuguese in the village were personally very clean. Their clothing was mended to perfection. A lot of the men's work clothes were so patched it was hard to recognize the original cloth of the garment. The men had clean work clothes at the beginning of each week; clean because of the communal washhouse.

The washhouse was characterized by a roof over what looked like a good-sized, raised swimming pool. Every time we drove by the building, the women would be gathered around this enormous tub, slapping and scrubbing the clothes vigorously, laughing and chattering away like magpies. The clothes, once dealt with in the tub, were draped on every available piece of fence or ground, to bleach or dry. The children of these women were either in school or playing outside the washhouse where their mothers could keep an eye on them.

Every Monday we would meet these women riding their donkeys home from Estoril or Cascais, the donkeys laden with the laundry. How serene they seemed, as they rode their donkeys in a leisurely fashion, never making the animal go any faster than it cared to. I swore I would get a donkey to ride to the market so I could have an excuse to take all day at the job.

It was difficult to get Maria and Celita to take a day off

because they had nothing to do with their leisure. But let a fiesta come along! Any kind of a fiesta; any excuse for a fiesta, and what happiness and anticipation! All work was rushed and finished before their good clothes were donned for the party. The best part of the fiesta, of course, was the anticipation. Maria and Celita would be all smiles from the moment they learned their husbands were taking them to the fiesta. I was amazed to discover these wives did not know whether they would go to the fiesta with their husbands until the very last moment. They suffered hours of anxiety wondering whether their spouses would go to the fiesta by themselves, or allow them to accompany them.

Of social life in Portugal we had little. The Latins are slow to invite strangers into their homes. And in any case we are not great visiting people ourselves. Portuguese women of the better class seem to be confined to their households by their husbands. The bars and night clubs late at night are almost entirely populated by males, who sit in dark clothing, like so many crows on a fence, drinking wine and brooding over whatever it is that makes the upper-class Portuguese seem so sad.

In the afternoons, however, the women go shopping, which means they spend hours drinking tea in very English tea-shops. They are dressed like strollers in the Easter parade on Fifth Avenue, and eat huge quantities of delightful little cakes, horribly fattening, stuffed with cream and almond paste and jam. I ate lots of them myself.

What did we do in the evenings? We had coffee before the fireplace in the living room, and listened to the radio—there are excellent broadcasts of classical music from the Lisbon station—and we read to each other.

It was heavenly. No busses thundered outside the house, no neon lights desecrated the darkness. There was only the warmth of the fire, and outside, the mountains and the pine forests, and beyond them, the rolling Atlantic, pale and yet majestic in the starlight.